Techno-Chop

THE NEW BREED OF CHOPPER BUILDERS

Mike Seate

With photography by Simon Green & Steve Terry

MOTORBOOKS

First published in 2005 by Motorbooks, an imprint of MBI Publishing Company, Galtier Plaza, Suite 200, 380 Jackson Street, St. Paul, MN 55101-3885 USA

Motorbooks titles are also available at discounts in bulk quantity for industrial or sales-promotional use. For details write to Special Sales Manager at MBI Publishing Company, Galtier Plaza, Suite 200, 380 Jackson Street, St. Paul, MN 55101-3885 USA.

ISBN 0-7603-2116-7

Editor: Peter Schletty
Designer: Mandy Iverson

Printed in China

Front cover photos by Michael Lichter
Frontis photo by Simon Green
Title page photo by Steve Terry
Back cover photos by Simon Green (left), Mike Seate (right), and Dain Gingerelli (top)

CONTENTS

FOREWORD

I'm European. More accurately, I'm English.

It's not an apology, though some say it should be. The point is that in England, choppers are so rare they may as well not exist.

My earliest motorcycle recollection was holding my dad's hand while waiting to cross the street, as a Norton Commando and a Triumph Bonneville raced each other off the stoplight in front of us. The aggressive noise, and the blinding reflection of the elusive English sun off chrome and metalflake paint somehow never left me. When I was old enough to ride, the Japanese had long since stolen the performance crown, and I rode big sportbikes just like my friends. Even now it's still all about the fastest new bike every season. Maybe it's a peculiarly English thing, linked to the type of roads available, but pretty well everybody rides a sportbike. I always knew choppers existed, but I don't think I'd ever seen one "in the flesh" until I moved to the United States. I guess I'd always imagined choppers and Harleys as the same things, which to me were slow bikes ridden by older guys, with beards.

When Mike Seate asked me to shoot some choppers for his new book, I happily agreed. Mike writes great books and it would be a fun change from shooting sportbikes. In secret I was a little concerned I wouldn't understand my subject matter, so I started to immerse myself into this new world. I quickly realized that in American culture these bikes are simply everywhere.

It's not difficult right now to gain insight into the chopper scene. You turn on the TV any night of the week and there's a show on about the bikes and their builders. There are as many magazines devoted to them as there are to sportbikes back in Europe. I'm the foreign guy, so while I don't know how it grew to be this big, big it is. I learned very quickly that my preconceived ideas were far from reality.

The first bikes I shot were built by Jason Grimes from Northeast Chop Shop in Maine. I immediately started to "get it." First, Jason is a great ambassador for the scene; second, the bikes turned out to be intriguing. I was given a tour of the workshop at NCS, and the first thing I saw was an oil tank being made from sheet metal. I mean *handmade* from basically nothing to going onto somebody's dream bike. I immediately realized the appeal I'd never seen: Everything is either handmade or carefully chosen for the current project bike.

Unlike other bikes that are made in production runs, where you have a couple of color choices to make you feel unique, these really *are* unique. Every bike has its own theme, its own flavor. Even parts that are produced in quantity get changed in some way for the customer, or painted to suit.

The details won me over. Every bike I shot for this book was different from the next, and as I write this foreword, weeks after shooting the last bike, I can still vividly remember those details. I have none of my own images to look at, yet I can picture perfectly in my head the mirrors and bar-ends that Dave Perewitz made for the Aerosmith bike, the engraved "insult" hidden in the depths of the matte black NCS bobber, the suicide shifter on the Jester bike.

I think this is what people grow so passionate about when they own these machines. Every little part of that bike is theirs, rarely interchangeable with any other bike out there. The builder includes more of the owners' personality than even a custom surfboard maker can.

This is what I attempted to portray with my images. The bikes look awesome when viewed as a whole, with their graceful flowing lines, but I think they look even more impressive when you lock in on just one part, something unique to that machine. It can be an area of glistening chrome engine parts nestling together, or the glint of metalflake paint on a stretched gas tank. The details that took me back to that Brit bike street race I watched as a kid. The Norton won that race, and I now have a Commando in the back of my garage, other bikes have come and gone while it's kept its spot. I won't sell it, as it's probably responsible for me riding bikes.

Now I find myself contemplating a chopper, though I don't know where I'd start for a "theme." Maybe that's the wrong way of looking at it, maybe that's what the builder does for you, but it's a world of choices compared to investing money into any other bike out there. I do know a theme of cameras and lenses would look really cheesy. . . .

On to cameras and lenses. In 2004 everybody is surprised to see a photographer loading film into a camera. It's funny that digital has grown so much in popularity that film causes a reaction. Digital is essential for some jobs, and faultless for snaps of my new family, but film is far from dead. It's been evolving for 100 years; that's at least 90 years more than digital has, so it still has its uses, and I suspect always will.

This book was shot solely on film. Some of the vivid color shots you'll see in here could have only been shot with film. For those who are interested, I used a Nikon F5 for this project, with a 24-120 VR lens, a 70-200 VR and a good old-fashioned 50-mm too.

Maybe the camera equipment is comparable to the subject of the book, both have a lineage that you can easily trace back in time. And both use the best of modern technology to function as effectively as possible, the best combinations of old and new.

I had a lot of fun shooting this book. From the gang members' bikes shot at rallys, to Brad Whitford from Aerosmith coming along in his own time to give the Aerosmith bike an extra touch of authenticity. The people in the chopper world are cool. I don't mean *trying* to be cool, I mean they are cool. They are fun, friendly, helpful, organized, and passionate about their world. If you try and come up with something comparable, anything else you can have handmade for you in such a personalized way, you can see just why they are so passionate. It's not just the bikes that are unique—their scene is unique, and that's the binding agent.

I've been inspired. I guess the best endorsement from me is that I can't wait to shoot the next book. I've got a head full of images that I can't wait to put on paper, and a seemingly infinite choice of bikes, builders, and owners. Enjoy the book, especially you "converts" like me.

—Simon Green

INTRODUCTION

For a style of motorcycle very recently considered passé, the unprecedented growth of the custom chopper industry is one of transportation's true miracles. In an age when motorcycles have become lighter, faster, and technologically more complex, choppers (which are, by nature, a decidedly anti-technology statement) are more popular than ever.

It goes without saying that much of the Zeitgeist surrounding long, low, and stripped-down motorcycles is due to their almost ubiquitous presence on television; programs such as the Discovery Channel's beloved *American Chopper* and *Monster Garage* series have managed to put choppers into the living rooms of middle-America with a thoroughness that master builders such as Arlen Ness and Dave Perewitz never dreamt of. As a result, the general public now regards customized motorcycles with the same affinity previously reserved for NASCAR drivers, NFL stars, and whoever won this season's round of *American Idol*. Miniature radio-controlled versions of Jesse James' rawboned choppers can now be purchased in the toy departments of your friendly neighborhood Wal-Mart, and burly bikers who just a few years ago were considered an arch threat to decent family values are now being heralded by the mainstream media like conquering heroes.

During the last year, more times than I can honestly recall, soccer moms and elderly shoppers have approached me in mall parking lots and pleaded for a photo of themselves or their kids posed near my own chopper; it's not hard to recall a time just 20 years ago when parents steered their kids away from a motorcyclist. Approaching one for a photo op was about as unimaginable as strangers inviting us over for a family dinner.

But with the mainstreaming of choppers among the non-riding public comes a small but inevitable backlash from the very mechanics, artisans, and backyard builders who keep the craft of creating custom motorcycles alive and well away from the spotlight. To the new breed of chopper riders and builders, the high-concept, six-figure show choppers occupying so much of prime-time television are as far removed from the reality of what's being ridden on the streets that *American Chopper* might as well be bolting together motorcycles to run on another planet. The chopper and its soulful precursor the bob-job were borne not out of a Hollywood TV producer's puerile imagination, but in the back alley shed of a bunch of grease-caked, empty-pocketed mechanics who were simply obsessed with taking a bone-stock motorcycle and recreating it to resemble something closer to their own aesthetic vision. It didn't take months of intense marketing research, focus groups, or vertically integrated sales formulas; it was all about welding torches and hacksaws, and that insatiable search to be cooler than the next throttle jockey cruising down the boulevard.

In the three years since my first book on the history and development of custom motorcycles was published, I've witnessed a wild, almost frenzied ride for builders to out-design and overreach the man or woman in the next service bay. But what has proven the most exhilarating and inspiring is how many chopper builders are still out there, wholly uninfluenced by the big-money craze

of the mainstream chopper scene. Again and again, we've come across small, backstreet chopper chops where fabricators are deriving pleasure from creating eye-pleasing motorcycles for all the right reasons. They aren't hoping to grab a seat next to Jay Leno on NBC's *Tonight Show* or see their faces adorning light beer cans. They build choppers because they're interesting means of expressing one's self through mechanical artistry, and they're one hell of a blast to ride.

This is not to suggest that established, well-respected, chopper builders have lost sight of what's real. Along the way, we ran into veteran builders such as Dave Perewitz, owner of Bridgewater, Massachusetts' Cycle Fabrications and saw how a venerable chopper wizard keeps abreast of the latest trends, and we saw that money, fame, and notoriety is in no way a detriment

to the flow of ideas that keeps the chopper industry bubbling. We met a true eccentric artist in Connecticut's Tommy Imperati, a wildly creative chopper enthusiast who has blended his love of the gunsmithing trade with custom motorcycles for some breathtaking results. We found some of the first female chopper designers and plenty of talented young upstarts who are bringing influences and fabrication techniques to the scene that would have been tough to visualize just a decade previously.

Over in Europe, where the chopper was kept alive through technological innovation during the 1980s when most American builders were caught up in the (mercifully) short-lived fat bike craze, a new generation of craftsmen are proving that potential overexposure is no detriment to creativity. The streetfighter, a stripped-down, utilitarian, and high-performance cousin to the chopper that was

borne of the sportbike scene, is also making inroads into the world of choppers both here and abroad, proving that the old barriers to custom bikes are fast fading. Builders are incorporating elements from the performance biking scene such as inverted front forks; low-profile, wide radial tires; and multi-piston brakes as a means of matching a chopper's radical looks with equally formidable performance.

And just as everything old becomes new again, we've watched in awe as imported motorcycles— from the new generation of water-cooled Triumph machines from Great Britain to the racetrack-ready

V-Twins designed by Eric Buell—have found their way into choppers, just as the Honda 750-four and Kawasaki's formidable Z-1 engines did a good 30 years ago.

Overall, what we witnessed was something akin to a return to the basics of chopper building's past. Designers are more focused on keeping things simple and functional rather than rending metal into some sort of rolling tribute to abstract concepts and science-fiction-fantasy-poster art. For every $6,000 TIG-welded chassis on sale at a top-end custom shop, there's some ambitious builder armed with a hacksaw, a jar of Bondo putty, and

Author Mike Seate

a spray can determined to prove a real chopper can still be as much about passion as it is price. Some 60 years after returning WWII veterans began chopping parts from their stock Harley-Davidsons, Indians, and British bikes to make them perform better and look more stylish, and 30 years after choppers reached a strange baroque stage with the stretch bikes popular during the 1960s, choppers in this new age have come again to represent nothing more than a builder, a vision, and an enjoyment of riding something different than the guy down the block. Keep it real.

Mike Seate

chapter 1

THE STATE OF CHOPPER NATION

In the summer of 2004, I noticed something about biking that I'd never witnessed in 26 years of riding streetbikes. Whenever I took to the road on one of my two-wheelers, people seemed to like me. And it didn't really matter whether it was my two-year-old West Coast Chopper, a beautiful exercise in mechanical creativity and undeniably bad-ass street cred that I'd had constructed by Steve Peffer of Pittsburgh's Steel City Choppers, or one of my high-performance Italian sportbikes. Everyone from grandmothers to college students to laborers working on road repair crews smiled, waved, or gave me a thumbs-up sign. This was quite a different reception than I'd received when I first started riding motorcycles in the late 1970s. Back then, if someone bothered to notice a passing biker, it was usually to stare in disapproval. Or it was a police officer sizing up your likely illegal custom bike for a few equipment violations.

With choppers all the rage, even old-school machines like this early 1970s Shovelhead are being rolled out of musty garages, rebuilt, and ridden.

Ah, but here we are in the age of the celebrity chopper builder and near 24-hour TV coverage of custom motorcycles, an age where mothers wear Orange County Choppers T-shirts to kids' soccer games and the store shelves at the local Wal-Mart are stocked deep with mini-chopper toys. To experience this phenomenon firsthand is to witness the power of television as a medium capable of dictating the country's tastes in popular culture. It also speaks volumes about how motorcycles, previously thought of as dangerous toys for tough guys and nihilists, had been transformed into something akin to a family fun vehicle, a two-wheeled oddity like the Oscar Meyer Weinermobile that Dad and the kids could enjoy on equal terms. If I parked the West Coast Chopper at a biker hangout, I experienced the same weird phenomenon again and again; riders clamoring for a glimpse of the famously designed chopper, and some even brought along their kids and cameras, hoping for evidence of a piece of American folklore they could share with future generations

But even at a time when West Coast Choppers and its trademark Maltese cross logo are more synonymous with motorcycling than even the bar and shield of Harley-Davidson, stretched, raked, and bobbed motorcycles themselves remain something of a rarity in this day and age. Or at least the type of big-bucks choppers that helped push their once-marginalized form of mechanical art to the forefront of pop culture consciousness.

These motorcycles, while glaringly present in the public's imagination, have somehow, perhaps due to their astronomical expense, become almost like consumer icons rather than everyday transportation. While tens of thousands of riders tool around on stock motorcycles or bikes modified by bolt-on aftermarket accessories, many hold a Matt Hotch chopper or a one-off from the Huntingdon Beach garage of Chica in their hearts and minds as the ultimate dream machine. Visit biker gatherings in most cities and actual choppers are thin on the ground. Like the hot rod car movement that started in the 1950s, true lead sled custom cars have now

Wide rear tires—now up to a lane-splitting 330 millimeters—are said to be the current chopper movement's extended forks, meaning too much is never enough!

become such baroque exercises in overindulgence and rich man's fantasy, it's truly rare to see a 1957 Chevy or a three-door Ford coupe driven on the roads other than when they're being driven to a vintage car cruise or concourse show. And though these classic cars maintain a steady fascination for the general public, out on the streets where the rubber hits the road, the closest thing to a hot rod rumble you'll see involves not $150,000 in restored antique Americana, but legions of younger folks, stripping down and tuning out affordable late-model import cars. In doing so, they've created a workingman's alternative to the traditional hot rod scene, one full of innovation, new ideas, and adrenaline-fueled excitement.

Likewise, even though the majority of TV-star choppers tend to be constructed of unobtanium, that most precious of metals, it hasn't stopped inventive builders from coming up with clever and affordable ways to chop cheaper machines. In fact,

just the opposite seems to be happening. Faced with the desire to ride a machine that represents the cutting edge of custom motorcycle design on a limited budget, chopper fanatics the world over are donning welding goggles, busting out the hacksaws, and adopting a do-it-yourself approach to choppers that's revitalizing the scene itself.

"I get people riding their bikes to my shop every day, all excited about some fancy chopper they saw on TV the night before, asking me to make their stock Harley Fatboy look and ride like one of those bikes," explains Sara Liberte, a female chopper builder from the East Coast. "I always try and tell them there's just no way they can have both at the same time. Those Discovery Channel bikes can't be ridden all day or cross-country and anything with that much chrome and detailing isn't going to look that way for long if you actually get out there and ride it."

With several dozen custom project builds under her belt, Liberte says today's custom motorcycle builders have to concentrate on crafting motorcycles that are visually stunning and innovative in their design, while also staying mechanically sound and capable of being ridden all day.

"What good is a beautiful $120,000 motorcycle if the front end is so long it won't go around a corner, or it's so valuable it would get stolen if you parked it anywhere?" she asks.

These recent developments in the custom biking community are coincidental, considering that this is just where the custom motorcycle market found itself about halfway through the initial chopper craze that swept this country in the late 1960s and early 1970s. Choppers, having evolved out of the post-WWII bobber tradition where parts were simply shed from stock motorcycles to enhance their performance, had slowly morphed into little more than rolling pieces of abstract sculpture over a couple of decades.

Technology struggles to keep pace with the fertile imagination of chopper builders such as Bill Steele of Pennsylvania's Oakdale Custom Cycles.

Car shows and early custom motorcycle competitions such as the annual Rat's Hole gathering on the boardwalk at Daytona Beach became rife with extravagantly designed, immaculately finished show choppers, many of which were ridden only to the shows or into a studio for a manicured photography shoot in a lifestyle magazine. Some

The single-sided swingarm was adopted from superbikes such as Ducati's legendary 916. The oil tank on this Oakdale chopper is mounted fore of the engine, helping to keep things running cool.

never held oil in their cylinders or gas in the fuel tanks at all, spending their time getting ferried from show to show in the backs of padded trailers. While most of the custom vehicle fans in the general public (the folks who had brought the kids along to a World of Wheels Weekend show to see George Barris' Batmobile and the Banana Splits' groovy, psychedelic van from the popular Saturday morning children's program) found these über-choppers a delight to behold, many a biker couldn't have been more turned off if they'd just spied Zsa Zsa Gabor's pink Alfa Romeo displayed on a bed of pink cashmere sweaters.

As a result, many a back-alley chopper fan turned away from the bikes in the limelight, dismissing them as too rich, too over-the-top, and, to be honest, just too fragile to be ridden on anything like a regular basis. This unexpected backlash provided the motivation and impetus for the dozens of early chopper parts aftermarket houses that today are household names. Manufacturers such as Jammer Enterprises, Drag Specialties, and A.E.E.

Choppers managed to offer riders cheap and, in many cases, well-constructed components that made anyone with a shop bench and a toolbox capable of creating their own streetable chopper.

So, if the top-flight show choppers are too expensive for the average throttle jockey to afford, why do we still find them so fascinating? Well, that depends upon whom you ask. Some say the popularity of choppers can be traced to America's newfound respect for blue-collar workers and craftspeople in general; with most of our manufacturing jobs now exported overseas, there's an inherent national pride in something as mechanically unique as a customized motorcycle, a concept as uniquely American as muscle cars. It's the same feeling of pride and respect for mechanical innovation many people feel when watching a military air show. Sure, not many of us will ever get close to the cockpit of an F-18 fighter jet, but they're damn cool to look at. And just as everyday sportbike riders will dress themselves in the livery of their favorite superbike racers while never venturing near a roadrace circuit, riders of stock or bolt-on cruisers feel a natural affinity for the more outrageous chopper designs, which, in time will work their way into the motorcycles we see and purchase from the showroom floor.

This desire to make choppers affordable and accessible to larger numbers of riders is not lost on the big-name builders, however. Like fashion designers who create wildly expensive and frequently shocking ware for runway shows, the millionaire chopper set often uses its high-dollar, high-concept showbikes to test-market ideas to the general public via the custom shows and glossy chopper magazines. What doesn't fly with the public is very often excised from the design table, but ideas such as piked updraft air cleaners, single-sided swingarms, 120-spoke wire wheels, and air-ride suspension systems are eventually made available to the general public through marketing deals with the big aftermarket houses.

Sometimes, it's mainstream custom bike riders who favor the more outrageous designs. When Avon introduced the 200 series rear radial tire for custom motorcycles a scant decade ago, many felt the 5.5-inch-wide rim was too broad to offer stable handling. Ten years later, the desire to build choppers with ever-wider rear tires continues unabated, like a bodybuilder's quest for bigger and badder muscles. Though most experienced motorcycle test riders and even a few chopper pilots will attest to the fact that an 8- or 9-inch-wide rim mated to a 2.25-inch-wide front tire will cause more flop than a new season of network sitcoms, today's aftermarket offers chopper builders the option of 300-millimeter, and now even 330-millimeter, rear radials. And to think psychologists used to liken a chopper's extended forks to devices for male sexual overcompensation!

All this "build on Sunday, sell on Monday" stuff offers a quick, ruthless cycle of research, design, development, and sales, which only appears to be growing larger and more influential by the month. Jesse James builds a café racer prototype for Honda Motorcycles using its own thudding 1,800-cc VTX motor. A street version is soon rumored to be in the works. Master chopper builders Arlen and Cory Ness are drafted into service to revitalize the less-than-inspiring V-Twins offered by Minnesota's Victory Motorcycle Company, and the results of their Victory Vegas and Hammer cruisers are increased sales and a cache of cool among custom bike enthusiasts the world over. Can it be long before designer versions of popular street cruisers are available, imprinted with the inimitable labels of popular chopper builders? In a way, they already are.

Quick and nimble, this chopper utilizes a Buell S-1 Lightning motor and streetfighter styling—nice!

Pick up the current catalog from California's Custom Chrome, Inc., and the phone book–sized tome reads like a fashion supplement from a big city department store for all its cache of designer labels and instantly recognizable high-end goods. Frames and fenders are available from many of the custom chopper craftsmen made popular on TV, as are lines of designer chopper duds that let you dress like your heroes as well. Of course, the main thing amateur builders want from these wish books is cheaper parts that will hold up to the rigors of everyday use. To that end, the big builders have more than delivered. Once purchased, many amateur chopper mechanics set out to alter or, in their eyes, improve upon the designs of an old-school master builder, adding sheetmetal details to fenders and gas tanks, and altering the width and rake of designer frames.

"I really dig choppers because I think they're some of the coolest, most radical motorcycles on the planet," explains Kai Morrison of South Dakota's Twisted Choppers. "But when you're my age, the only way you're gonna get your hands on

one is to either win the lottery or build a cheaper version on your own using whatever parts you can afford or can make yourself." Not even old enough to have lived through the first chopper craze, Morrison's bikes, ironically, are built with much of the raw, purposeful feel of the original choppers. He's far from alone. From the former Czech Republic to Germany, the United Kingdom, and the United States, choppers are attracting a new generation of enthusiasts, many of whom have few, if any, ties to the traditions and designs of the past.

Some will prophesize that choppers are closely related to the streetfighter, an equally stripped-down streetbike style that originated in the United Kingdom and Europe during the early 1990s. The streetfighter, with its exposed engine, bizarre paint schemes, and dirt-track handlebars, was created mostly from the road-scarred remains of crashed high-performance sportbikes. It is slowly making its presence known through custom bikes being built by new-school artists such as Tom Langton of Canada's Rumble Customs and Seattle's Russ Tom who seamlessly blends sportbikes with

17

Skulls, like tattoos and leather, will never go out of style for chopper enthusiasts.

choppers to dazzling effect. You can see it in the upside-down forks, the single-sided swingarms, and the dual headlights, and feel it through the use of race-tuned engines in choppers with short wheelbases and multiple, drilled disc brakes.

As choppers continue to emerge as a more worldwide phenomenon, international influences will, thankfully, continue to alter what's considered a correct chopper. At this point, it all depends on where you point your front wheel and who you're talking shop with. In Germany, for example, the chopper has long struggled to gain a market ruled by restrictive federal transportation laws governing the length of front forks and the height of handle-bars. They've also struggled with the prohibitive

costs of imported Harley-Davidson motorcycles to use as donor bikes. Ohio's Led Sled Customs, on the other hand, routinely peruses salvage yards for offbeat motorcycle engines to use in their hard-edged, no-frills custom choppers, including a water-cooled, three-cylinder motor from one of the new Triumph motor corporation's Daytona 900 sportbikes. The old Triumph line, out of production since 1982, is also beginning to re-emerge as a choice powerplant for many new-school chopper builders. The beloved parallel twin's legendary torque and ease of maintenance—not to mention the fact that an old Bonneville engine can be had for as little as the cost of a billet aluminum wheel from a top-flight custom catalog—have all helped this unlikely retro machine in its comeback.

Today, German custom shops such as Hamminkeln's Thunderbike are turning to choppers crafted from Japanese motorcycles for a creative outlet. Stylized by a relatively short front end but sturdy well-crafted chassis and bodywork components, Thunderbikes have capitalized on the growing popularity of so-called "metric cruisers" such as Yamaha's Road Star line by offering complete chopper kits for the big-inch Asian twins. Built with typical German quality and technical know-how, Thunderbike's choppers cover a broad spectrum of custom options, from bobber look-alike kits that widen and lower the profile, to stretch choppers-in-a-box for the more adventurous. They offer the home-builder a chance to take an otherwise unremarkable Japanese cruiser, say, a Suzuki Intruder 1400, and, with a few well-placed components, turn it into something that can hold its own among the Softail Deuces and Sportster Customs parked along Main Street.

The metric chopper scene is also taking flight, albeit in a more prototype form, in the United States as well. Aftermarket parts heavyweight Cobra Engineering has enlisted the skills of Denny Berg, one of the Midwest's most talented motorcycle customizers, to create high-end parts for metric cruisers and some of the one-off machines. Berg has provided proof that a motorcycle's country of origin has little to do with its potential to make a great chopper. Berg, however, is operating in the rarefied air of the research and development chopper builder, working with decades of sheetmetal skill and a project budget that would have Bay Area veteran Ron Simms remortgaging his house.

Rightfully, there are those in the chopper world who contend that money, especially the six-figures a hand-built chopper can demand, is good for business and innovation. With unlimited research dollars comes freedom of creativity. When a Hank Young or Jesse Jurrens can spend months testing the oscillation and chatter rate on a set of hand-welded girder forks or the ability of a one-off, hand-pounded, aluminum gas tank to hold fuel, it will eventually translate into safer and cheaper parts for the rider on the street.

"On one hand, you have all these millionaire builders stealing the limelight with these bikes no real person can afford, but you can't deny that they're stunning to look at and incredible in terms of sheer craftsmanship," says Howard Kelly, a veteran chopper rider and former editor of *Hot Bike* magazine. "Then again, the kind of money it takes to make a chopper like that alienates the 28-year-olds who just want to own and ride a cool-looking bike. But don't make the mistake of assuming that money hasn't been good for the custom bike industry, all around. It's brought in a better type of client, made the custom shows more family friendly and, let's face it, little old ladies are a lot less likely to be afraid of somebody on a big, loud motorcycle these days than they were, say, 25 years ago."

Kelly, who left the magazine in late 2004, makes an interesting point. Without the Dave Perewitzs and Mitch Bergerons of the world cranking out immaculate, high-concept show choppers, the customer demand that fuels the worldwide hunger for choppers may not exist at all. To that end, the high-end, celebrity chopper builders have upped the ante, pressing themselves to build motorcycles that, even in today's highly competitive custom bike scene, are still amazing to conceive. It doesn't take a long look at a chopper built by a veteran shop such as Milwaukee Iron or Don Hotop to realize that the

Motorcyclists often stare death in the face, but few as frequently as the rider on this wacky machine.

technological and design boundaries these guys constantly approach, and subsequently surpass, has fueled the aftermarket parts explosion, the metric cruiser market, and thousands of imitators.

"Look, people grouse sometimes saying you guys are all TV stars now and your machines don't reflect what's happening on the street. But all my bikes are built to be ridden, just like they have been for the past 25 years," says Dave Perewitz. "There's nothing I like more than seeing what these young guys are doing with very little money, and we all talk shop and influence each other." True that.

Perewitz' choppers, bobbers, and custom low-riders started off in the 1970s with a combination of street-legal fork and frame dimensions and mind-blowing detailing. Not much has changed about that winning formula to date. He still wows the crowds with a liberal application of gold metalflake and voluptuously sculpted bodywork, and newcomers such as Russ Tom readily cite the jovial New Englander as an influence. And it nearly goes without saying that today's well-known celebrity bike builders all started off the way today's low-buck rebels did, building motorcycles in small garages not for fame, money, or international recognition, but for the love of the art. And say what you will about the shelves filled with chopper-based toys at your local Wal-Mart, the Orange County Choppers men's cologne for sale at upscale department stores, or the fact that Jesse James is more famous and easily recognized today than his

Though modern choppers are a lot more stable and safe on the road, owners still enjoy parking them up for a show-and-tell.

Simon Green

sort of genius-level innovation and brilliant technical expertise expected from builders with 20 or 30 years of experience.

The Chop Rod, as Tefft branded the bike, was constructed with a huge bow-shaped frame backbone in which four quarts of fuel for the 124-cubic-inch engine is stored. The triangular, almost insect-like, gas tank—which actually holds the engine lubricant—could hold its own in any avant-garde sculpture gallery.

Tefft formed Jolly Roger Customs, a limited-production chopper manufacturing company, around his first complete motorcycle and says he loves to work with what he describes as "unexpected materials," which explains the use of a tiny monoshock suspension system from a Cannondale mountain bicycle supporting the narrow leather solo seat, and a red anodized jockey shifter made from the parachute lever of a top-fuel dragster. A tiny halogen headlight tops off a set of chromed Goldammer forks, and the weird flat handlebars employ one of French builder Cyril Huze's internal throttles. But Tefft was determined to employ the same time-consuming and ultimately rewarding personal touches as the builders he idolizes from television, having hand-bent the stubby coal-black exhaust system in his workshop where he also fabricated the machine's spare sheetmetal components and chassis.

Tefft may not have started out with a huge budget behind him and, like many chopper fanatics spurred on by what they're seeing in mass media, he made some considerable personal financial sacrifices in order to make his dream of becoming a motorcycle builder a reality. When low-end chopper makers complain that money may be an evil influence on the scene, they have to remember that even if Tefft charges a customer upwards of $50,000 for his machine, he will never come close to compensating

motorcycles, the chopper boom has, in a way, fueled motorcycling's notoriety and creativity in ways that are difficult to measure.

Take Milford, Michigan's Derrin Tefft, for example. Tefft had never considered riding a custom chopper, let alone building one, until he caught a broadcast of Discovery Channel's *Great Biker Build-Off* series, which inspired him to try his hand at fabricating a motorcycle basically from scratch. Taking a gander at Tefft's first foray into the chopper market belies his lack of experience. The glistening red stretch chopper he displayed at the Journey Museum during the 2004 Black Hills Classic motorcycle rally in Sturgis, South Dakota, was impressive enough to ride away with a Best In Show award. It also won Tefft a free trip to display the mean red chopper at the bi-annual Intermot motorcycle industry show in Munich, Germany. Despite it being a first effort, the machine was built with the himself fully for the countless man-hours and the sweat-equity invested in his custom chopper.

"These things are going to be expensive because they take so dang long to figure out and get rolling the right way," opines Chris Johnson, the head man at Carolina Custom Products, a Wilkesboro, North Carolina, chopper house that's been building its own brand of gracefully detailed and hugely powerful choppers since 1999. Before that, the firm, owned by industrialist Mike Archie, was busy producing some of the better high-end logging equipment on the U.S. market. Archie's personal stable of vehicles included several choppers, and some of his fellow riders were particularly interested in the CNC-machined billet aluminum wheels that the CCP crew had made on the firm's equipment. As so often happens, the occasional request for parts soon blossoms into a genuine side business and today CCP offers

20 different styles of custom billet wheels and choppers constructed around them.

Johnson and builder Dorian Swanner have lately turned their considerable skills toward the construction of chopper frames with a one-off custom rugged, low-profile pro-street design (known as the 38-6 for its rake and frame stretch dimensions) for those who like their choppers drag-strip fast, and a mile-long softail model with a tubular swingarm and 5 inches of stretch in the frame backbone. Out on the road, the wide 300-millimeter rear tires on these bikes are said to provide a very well-balanced ride thanks to the dense chrome-moly frame tubing and conservative trial measurements built into these machines, despite the lazy 46-degree rake of the orange softail chopper. "They'll run as true and comfortable as any factory Harley-Davidson, which is not an easy thing to do with a chopper," Johnson says.

A Texas chopper, characterized by its clean lines and long gas tank, is now available through a vast dealer network.

Often referred to as bar-hoppers for their short-range comfort, choppers are at home parked near any saloon.

The cost of a complete CCP bike runs anywhere from $35,000 to $40,000, but the main components are all from the top-flight aftermarket houses where quality and reliability is not an issue. "There are so many variables to consider when getting into a chopper if you're going to use it out on the road," explains Johnson, "so we prefer to use S&S engines exclusively because they're so reliable. We use all Baker 6-speed transmissions so you can kinda kick back in that top overdrive gear and just cruise, and we use either Pro-One forks or American Suspension upside-down forks, things that are proven and will hold up for a buyer with no worries. You have a hard time doing that with a chopper built from junkyard parts or entirely from scratch."

The real challenges for a firm like CCP that still uses a certain amount of off-the-shelf aftermarket equipment (the sheetmetal on both the silver and orange choppers are from Fat Katz, the exhausts from Grumpy's Customs) is the constant need to create new parts and designs that they may not run into at one of the 40 custom bike shows they enter each year. "When it comes to building choppers, the hardest part is trying to dream up something new and different from what everybody else is doing. You'll spend weeks working out an idea and go to a show and somebody you never met had the same damn idea," Johnson says, the frustration telling in his voice. The crew basically begins each project with a series of pencil sketches that they present to a customer for consultation and any

North Carolina's Redneck Engineering amazed the crowds at the Myrtle Beach Rally with this wicked, and very spidery, single-loop chopper. The frame, along with the rail-thin elliptical gas tank, will eventually be made available to legions of Redneck dedicated fans.

possible changes in rake, trial, wheels, etc. From there, it's on to the shop's small assembly line where the motorcycle takes shape over the course of several months.

So far CCP has set up a dealer network with about 50 representatives located in the United States and Canada, but Johnson says requests are starting to roll in from around the world. This is pretty heady stuff for a bunch of guys who, just a few years ago, were churning out tree saws and wood lathes, but they don't seem particularly surprised. Though it can take awhile to locate the right buyer for one of CCP's high-end custom projects, Johnson says the switch from working on logging equipment to designing choppers has been a wonderful one. "People always ask me what the difference is between what I used to do and what I do now, and I tell them I enjoy coming to work now," he laughs.

Sometimes, it's a family connection and plenty of imagination that helps get a foot through the door of the custom bike-building community. Lynn Chambers of Myrtle Beach, South Carolina, didn't have a bankroll the size of a stroker piston, a well-known face, or, at the age of 18, much of a history with choppers. What he did have was his grandfather, Richard Silvey, who had spent the past three decades constructing some of the South's most respected high-performance antique cars. It was in the family garage that Chambers, now 24, learned his way around a TIG welder, English wheel, and lathe, providing the skills Chambers would need to launch 2-9 Choppers in 2001.

His first well-received project bikes involved the tried-and-true method of bolting together a rolling chassis custom bike from a stock Harley-Davidson supplied by a customer and parts purchased mainly from existing aftermarket houses and

established chopper building firms. Chambers, who admits he can rarely leave an existing motorcycle part in its stock condition, soon realized his own ideas for how a motorcycle should run and look were easily as good as those he was purchasing from the aftermarket.

"At that point, I realized that my grandfather had already taught me everything I needed to know about making my own parts, so I decided to build a chopper from the ground up. It really just kind of multiplied from there with people asking us to build them choppers before we even had a garage to do it in," he laughs.

Though Chambers and Silvey still prefer to purchase the chassis for their smooth-as-silk choppers from established builders such as Redneck Engineering and Grumpy's Customs, they've since graduated to hammering out their own sheetmetal parts, banding their own exhaust tubing, and making the Chambers family name known for more than custom cars. Their kicked-out and muscular blue custom stretch chopper was built in just six weeks in order to make the show circuit during Daytona Beach Bike Week. A Grumpy's frame with 48 degrees of rake is mated to a set of Pro-One forks with an additional 6 degrees of rake in the chrome Wide Glide triple trees. The multi-generational team at 2-9 took over from there, manufacturing the blue powder-coated handlebars with internal wiring, the slick one-piece rear fender that's molded into a side panel covering the swingarm that's equipped with a set of air shocks from Legends, and the close-hugging piked fenders.

Though this machine came together in remarkably short time, Chambers, who splits his days between studying for a business degree at South Carolina's Coastal University and the chop shop, says time isn't really an issue when it comes to creating two-wheeled art. "Completed, these bikes

may sell for $36,000 to maybe $48,000 each, but even that's not getting paid for every drop of sweat and ounce of effort I put into them, says Chambers. "When you consider how many hours we invest in getting the metal work to look and fit just right or how much actual work you have in bolting together a bike not just once in bare metal, but a second time with all the custom-built parts in place and the internal wiring running inside the bars and frame so it looks clean and runs good, its incredible," he says, clearly amazed at his own efforts.

But after an impressive 19 complete choppers have rolled out of the 2-9 garage in the first three years of business, Chambers would be remiss not to allow himself some much-deserved props for how well the work has been received. "Everywhere I go, people are shocked that I'm so young and running a chopper shop. They either don't take me seriously at first or think I'm just a parts gopher. But when they see the bikes they usually are all shocked and I end up selling every one we build," he laughs.

It seems 2-9's customers are split along age lines, with younger riders preferring the more radical, stretch choppers and the older guys favoring the pro-street look. Chambers says it's all a question of comfort and making an appearance. "The older guys used to ride rigids and they have the lower backs to show for it, while the guys my age, they want the long stretch bikes that attract all the girls down on the beach and get you noticed," he says.

The red lowboy bobber completed by 2-9 in 2003 was also a rush-job, going from the ground to rolling down the freeway in just under six weeks. Chambers says the idea for the intricate, three-dimensional sculpted sections along the gas tank and seat pan came from studying the works of other builders at shows, then deciding that such a thing hadn't yet been attempted. The

Steve Terry

Long respected as a manufacturer of high-quality chopper and pro-street frames, South Carolina's Grumpy's Customs proves they're about more than the sum of their cherished custom parts with this muscular dropped-chassis chopper.

unique star-shaped seat pan was particularly labor intensive, with dozens of hours spent hand-hammering out a rider's accommodations, and then carefully fabricating a raised fin to carry the pattern along across the top of the custom-made gas tank. "I definitely like anything I make to look completely different from the traditional way people would design things. If they're all making round seat pans, mine will have to be star-shaped," he says.

Fresh blood brings a new realm of ideas to the chopper game, and builders who are in Chamber's youthful age group seem to carry none of the preconceptions about what's allowed or what, if any, parameters exist for chopper builders as some of their more experienced contemporaries. Plus, they're young enough to still see the challenges of building a chopper from scratch to be fun, not work.

Steve Terry

Another example of Redneck Engineering's third-generation chassis emphasizes long flowing lines and an oil bag cleverly built into the rear fender. The rider's seating position places him or her just 20 inches over the pavement.

"My grandfather had done so many street rods and he taught me so much when I was just a kid that this seems like a lot of fun for me still, like putting together a scale-model kit. I never expected something I just figured all kids knew how to do would end up getting this big," says Chambers. "Every now and then I'll ride one of our bikes to class on a sunny day and all my fellow students are totally into it. They can appreciate that every chopper builder, from the backstreet guy to the master, is definitely an artist in his own right."

Though Chambers doesn't see many other chopper builders emerging from his Generation-Y demographic, he's very encouraging about the possibility of seeing other members of the X-Games crowd get involved. They have to be unafraid to learn new things, willing to get their hands dirty and, more important, he says, they need to know that nobody gets to be a top-class builder overnight. "Anybody who has a dream should follow this. They just need a pair of mechanic's gloves, some raw sheetmetal and go at it and start playing around and sooner or later, they'll get the shapes they like. Don't be afraid to quit and start over again because you will get it wrong before you get it right."

In the end, the street chopper scene ends up divided between those who worship at the altar of the big-bucks well-known masters and the young upstarts determined to do it their way on a shoestring budget. Together, both schools are creating some memorable, unique, and awe-inspiring choppers, something that anybody who has ever thrown a leg over a motorcycle can enjoy.

Mike Seate

Mike Seate

Mike Seate

JOLLY ROGER'S

BUILDER: Derrin Tefft

ENGINE: S&S

DISPLACEMENT: 124 cubic inches

EXHAUST: Owner

TRANSMISSION: Baker 6-speed

FORKS: Goldammer

CHASSIS: Derrin Tefft

DIMENSIONS: 42-degree rake

GAS TANK: Owner

FENDERS: Owner

SEAT: Owner

Steve Terry

2-9 CHOPPERS

BUILDER: Lynn Chambers

ENGINE: S&S

DISPLACEMENT: 113 cubic inches

EXHAUST: Bassani

TRANSMISSION: Rev Tech 6-speed

FORKS: Pro-One

CHASSIS: Grumpy's Customs

DIMENSIONS: 48-degree rake,
    6-inch out, 4-inch upward stretch

GAS TANK: 2-9

FENDERS: 2-9

SEAT: 2-9

SPECIAL FEATURES: Legends air-ride
    suspension w/on-board
    compressor

RED LOW BOY

2-9 CHOPPERS

BUILDER: Lynn Chambers

ENGINE: Rev Tech

DISPLACEMENT: 110 cubic inches

EXHAUST: Martin Bros.

TRANSMISSION: Rev Tech 6-speed

FORKS: Harley-Davidson Deuce

CHASSIS: War Eagle

DIMENSIONS: 42-degree rake,
5-inch outward stretch

GAS TANK: 2-9

FENDERS: 2-9

SEAT: 2-9

SPECIAL FEATURES: Hand-fabricated
seat pan, bodywork, handlebars

Steve Terry

Steve Terry

CAROLINA CUSTOM PRODUCTS

BUILDER: Casey McCreary

ENGINE: Kendall Johnson/S&S

DISPLACEMENT: 141 cubic
inches

EXHAUST: Grumpy's Customs

TRANSMISSION: Baker 6-speed

FORKS: Pro-One

CHASSIS: Carolina Custom
Products

DIMENSIONS: 46-degree rake,
5-inch stretch

GAS TANK: Fat Katz

FENDERS: (front) Fat Katz,
(rear) Russ Weinemont

SEAT: Danny Gray

Steve Terry

Steve Terry

Steve Terry

CAROLINA CUSTOM PRODUCTS

BUILDER: Carolina Custom
    Products

ENGINE: Kendall Johnson/S&S

DISPLACEMENT: 96 cubic inches

EXHAUST: Grumpy's Customs

TRANSMISSION: Baker 6-speed

FORKS: American Suspension

CHASSIS: Carolina Custom
    Products

DIMENSIONS: 44-degree rake,
    5-inch stretch

GAS TANK: Fat Katz

FENDERS: Fat Katz

SEAT: Highrollers

33

chapter 2

DOWN & DIRTY: LOW-BUCK CHOPPERS AND RAT bikes

A few years back, a local Harley-Davidson dealership staged a promotional raffle for a new motorcycle. A custom builder had taken a showroom-new FXR-S model and stripped it bare, replacing the stock finish with an outlandish, almost silly-looking, bright pink paint scheme. Themed upon the famous Pink Panther cartoon series, the Hog even featured a tiny panther within the headlight bucket and cartoons of the motorcycle's namesake along the gas tank.

Too clean to be a genuine rat but too gnarly for the showbike circuit, Mike Viverito's Harley Sportster is a classic example of the neo-rat chopper movement.

One young man ogling the motorcycle from the shop's parking lot had screwed up his face as if he'd smelled something funky. "If I win that bike, I'm gonna kick the forks out about a foot, thrown on some apehangers, and spray the whole thing flat black. The fenders, the wheels, even the seat. That would be cool," he said as if drifting off into his own, primer-colored daydream. Some 15 years later, I think of that young rider's low-concept idea for a custom chopper more then ever.

Looking at the product rolling out of some of the newer chopper shops around the country, it appears there's a kinship of sorts brewing among builders who'd rather ride something raw, nasty, and mean-looking than a motorcycle that could grace the exclusive pages of the *Robb Report*.

Though not necessarily what you'd call rat bikes—baroque rolling tributes to mechanical neglect; technical improvisation; and a more-is-more decorative sense that is as old, if not older than, choppers themselves—the new breed of under-finished custom bikes is just as groundbreaking. Popularized in enthusiast magazines such as *The Horse: Backstreet Choppers*, and England's *Back Street Heroes* and *100% Biker*, these machines have the simple utilitarian appearance of heavy construction equipment, while often incorporating high-tech innovations that would shame your average General Motors engineer.

Because of the high price charged for many popular aftermarket chopper parts, the new rat builders often invest countless hours scouring

Decked out in traditional, matte black and vivid, red hot rod livery, this chopped rigid Sportster proves it doesn't take money to look cool.

motorcycle parts swap meets for old custom parts discarded at the end of the previous chopper craze. Internet auctioneer eBay has blossomed with sellers dealing almost exclusively in new old stock parts such as hexagon-shaped oil and gas tanks, angled fenders, twisted leg chrome springer front ends, and funky-looking banana seats. Because vintage chrome so often tarnishes over time, the shiny stuff is frequently re-dipped and sent back into action.

Some of the neo-rat builders, however, are not scouring used parts bins or the Internet for inspiration; they're just looking for a different creative take on the chopper movement as a whole. Pat Patterson, owner and principal builder at Dayton, Ohio's Led Sled Customs, is a fine example of a new chopper artist making his own way. When faced with the question of how much chrome to use when preparing one of his stealthed-out choppers, for example, he simply paints over it. Patterson, who spent several years operating a long-distance trucking firm before turning his passions to chopper building, says the cost of chroming parts is largely responsible for the out-landish prices commanded by most one-of-a-kind custom bikes. "Just paint over it," he suggests candidly. "That way, you're not wasting time waiting on some chromer to deliver parts when you're almost finished with the project, and you can spend that money on something else."

Patterson's advice may sound unusual, or maybe even heretical, but when the 31-year-old set out to start his own chopper shop in late 2002, he said his first thought was to "buck the tide against what everybody else was doing." All that is typically chromed would be doused with several coats of heat-resistant black paint. Having mastered the complicated engineering necessary to create his own multi-purpose frame welding jig, Patterson could create a one-off chassis to fit just about any motorcycle engine a customer threw his way. And instead of worrying about beautiful heart-rending airbrushed murals, he "wanted the ugliest paint I could find." Located adjacent to Wright-Patterson Air Force Base, that shade turned out to be the ubiquitous olive drab military green found on trucks, clothes, and even housing around military installations.

Patterson dunked one of his best-known custom bikes in the Army's favorite shade of green, creating a wicked sharp-edged weapon of a chopper that's

Nice detailing on a neo-rat chopper makes a dollar-sign into a nifty brake pedal.

graced the pages of several custom magazines. Instead of a rigid or softail-style rear end, the bike features a monoshock suspension borrowed from a Yamaha YZF sportbike, suspending a rear wheel with no fender whatsoever. In the place of passenger's footpegs, Led Sled saw fit to adorn the rounded one-off swingarm with star-shaped drilled plates for footrests. Dangerously piked endcaps cover the frame hoop just behind the rider's solo seat and forward-facing handlebar tips while a mile-high jockey shifter lever pokes up like a cavalry pike from the Sportster engine's left side.

The project, like all of Led Sled's ground-up customs, involves lengthy design sessions with the customer, which result in dozens of preliminary sketches. From there, Patterson starts creating a frame in his custom jig, using the rake and seat-height descriptions the customer provides. With no set frame geometry to be concerned with, seat

Pat Patterson of Ohio's Led Sled Customs will someday make a fortune by creating choppers that fit the average workingman's budget.

heights, rake and trail dimensions, and even the height of a top frame rail can all be re-set or altered before the chassis begins construction.

"My original vision was to build stuff straight from my imagination. A lot of people come in wanting new rake on their stock frames and we can do that and even switch them from a stock frame to a single downtube," says Patterson, who was such a ceaseless tinkerer as a child, he'd tear apart his model trucks and re-build them into different configurations when bored.

Patterson is a true believer in the utility and strong pulling power of the smaller XL motors from Harley-Davidson, a line of powerplants he feels have been mostly neglected in today's chopper market. "I don't really see anyone else specializing

in Sportsters and I feel like they get overlooked most of the time. I give people like Arlen Ness credit for showing how cool customized Sportsters could be back when he was doing all that stuff with diggers and all sorts of raked-out Sportster choppers in the 1970s. People forget it now, but Sportsters were what guys could afford to chop up back then. Big Twins cost too much!" he says.

Sportsters pop up with alarming regularity in the new rat bike scene, with many builders stockpiling garages full of parts for the old Ironhead XLs, which ended their production run with the introduction of Harley's Evolution Sportster powerplant in 1985. Cheap to purchase and easier to repair than a John Deere tractor, the 61-cubic-inch motors shake like a

A typically scrappy Led Sled bike adorned with dangerous-looking spiked accessories, a late-model Harley-Davidson Sportster engine, and plenty of attitude. The King Sportster gas tank has been stretched and mounted, Frisco-style. The forks retain a steep 36-degree rake angle, while the chassis has a new stretched neck and backbone.

cocktail mixer at a bachelor party, but have a dedicated following for just those reasons.

Some chopper historians actually argue that rat bikes and unadorned simple customs actually share more in common with the roots of the custom motorcycle movement than most people imagine. The motorcycles seen in historical photos from the infamous 1947 Labor Day rally in Hollister, California, reflect a certain down-and-dirty sensibility, with weathered solo saddles, blacked-out chrome bits, and front ends sans fenders being the norm. The nation's love affair with expansive murals, chromed rims, and sky-high sissy bars

came nearly two decades later, by which time many purists felt choppers had already become too pretty to be functional (or, for that matter, very macho).

This sensibility was later echoed in choppers built by innovators in the many outlaw motorcycle gangs that populated the West Coast in the 1960s. Check out an old *Life* magazine article, and you'll swear these stripped-down choppers with their rubber fork gaiters, monochrome paint schemes, and dusty coatings of road grime were built to attend *The Horse* magazine's annual Smoke Out festival! The focus was on cheap transportation; on building motorcycles that were way different from the stock Hogs being ridden by cops and touring types; and that, in a pinch, could be dropped when ridden too hard (or while being chased by The Man) without the owner crying over thousands of dollars worth of ruined chrome and airbrush art.

The late New York chopper legend "Indian" Larry Desment once explained at great length how "anything that didn't make a motorcycle faster was simply to be chopped off. That's what makes for a true chopper," he was fond of saying. And though Larry's machines were adorned with their fair share of chrome detailing and custom paint, as an avid

This Shovelhead neo-rat owned by a Led Sled staffer looks more like a 1950s street rod than a twenty-first-century custom, thanks to a leopard-skin seat and white rubber grips.

old schooler, his machines bore more in common with the rat choppers than they did the painstakingly detailed work of many of his contemporaries.

Desment, who died in late 2004 after performing a rolling seat-stand at a New Hampshire motorcycle show in front of thousands of fans, once said that the biker clubs in his hometown of Coney Island,

New York, used to laugh at the kinds of motorcycles movie bikers rode. "All those fancy velvet seats and peace signs—nobody on the street that

How to create a custom chopper sensation for pocket change. This machine has had its frame altered with a weld-in gooseneck section, short shocks in the rear, and fork tubes 8 inches overstock. Badass looks for about the price of a designer chopper wheel!

Who says you need a Gold Card and a stock portfolio to ride a chopper? This 1970s XLCH Sportster from Bare Bones Choppers was completed with swap-meet second-hand parts, including a weld-on hardtail and wheels vulcanized from an FXRS. Odd kickstand, though!

we knew back then could afford that stuff. That was all Hollywood and people picked up on it later. We just rode what we could afford; sometimes it was British, sometimes it was Harleys or choppers powered by old Indian motors if you could find them. If we had any money to spend on our choppers, we'd use it to make our bikes go faster," he said.

True rat bikes, however, are still found occasionally among the chopper crowd, but they've evolved from their heyday in the mid-1970s, when machines such as Smitty's famous rat Harley-Davidson Knucklehead made appearances on then-popular TV shows such as NBC's *Real People* and were featured in the pages of *Easyriders* magazine. Bikes like these were about as far removed from their lacquer-covered, carefully maintained counterparts on the chopper scene as

a Bimota SB8R superbike is from a stock Harley Sportster; the accumulation of ephemera, non-motorcycle-related add-ons—from ladies' brassieres to tin ham cans used as air cleaners—made a rat bike what it was.

Many builders, if they could truly be called that, relished in the fact that, after a few years and a few thousand miles, the motorcycles buried beneath the raccoon tails, horned cow skulls, and coat after coat of flat black (or Rustoleum brown, or even Army regulation green) paint were barely discernible to the untrained eye. As an anti-conformist statement, rat bikes outdid even choppers as a mechanical middle finger raised against the spit and polish of motorcycling's status quo.

As is the case today with the neo-rat movement, many aficionados get a real kick out of adorning their machines with "accessories" that an upscale,

This rider created an eye-popping effect for his low-buck chopper using his imagination and plenty of Bondo putty. The three-dimensional skull graphic and color-matched rocker boxes are pure street cred.

high-profile chopper craftsman wouldn't dream of letting near a custom bike. It's not unusual to find porcelain faucet knobs employed as jockey-shifter handles, lengths of rusty chain forced into service as brake and shifter linkage, and even bedrolls or pillows employed as passenger "seats."

Hidden beneath the grime and apparent mechanical neglect, however, was often a fire-breathing beat of a machine, a trick Indian Larry Desment said was frequently employed to make easy pickings at drag strips for rat bike owners. "Everybody would assume a guy riding a true rat chopper didn't take care of his machine or that it

was always just a couple of miles away from a major seize-up or a breakdown. Meanwhile, I knew guys who built up some serious fast stroker mills for their rats and would blow everybody away, leaking oil and shedding parts down the strip." That odd collaboration of brute horsepower, subterfuge, and just letting the elements have their way with a chopper still manages to stay alive today, and has found a ready-made following among chopper fans who believe style and speed don't have to cost an arm and a leg.

With the aptly fitting name of Billy "Badass" Rogers, the owner of the East Coast's Bare Bones Choppers is another staunch believer that custom motorcycles don't have to cost more than an Ivy League education to draw a crowd. In fact, Rogers, an admitted Sportster fanatic, will proudly tell a potential customer that he can create a ground-up chopper for less than $10,000.

"What I'm really into is using all the old leftover parts that people leave at the customs shops after they tear stuff off their stock bikes to put on all kinds of expensive bolt-ons," says Rogers, whose nickname belies a friendly affable personality. "If you know how to work with stock parts, especially the older stuff from the AMF years of Harley-Davidson, you can really have fun creating unique parts for not a lot of money."

Having worked at Butler, Pennsylvania's Cycle Warehouse for several years overseeing inventory and sales of one of the East Coast's largest stockpiles of custom accessories from the 1970s doesn't hurt Rogers in his quest to make cool bikes cheaply, either. And just as bell-bottom jeans, original Volkswagen Beetles, and Led Zeppelin records tend to hold a certain inexplicable fascination for kids too young to have witnessed them the first time around, most of the followers of the new rat bike scene are twenty- and thirty-somethings,

kids too broke to lust after a $100,000 custom chopper and too cool to really care about attaining one. "I know when I go to a show there's gonna be all kinds of expensive 'look-at-me' bikes that draw a crowd all day. But I threw on a set of green sport-bike radials from tomahawk tires and some other day-glow green stuff on this funky little rigid project chopper and suddenly everybody's headed over here. The difference is, they can actually afford one of my bikes," Rogers says with a laugh.

Some builders tackling the task of creating a chopper from a Harley-Davidson Sportster engine actually enjoy the relative scarcity of custom parts available for their favorite powerplant. Though most of the big custom parts suppliers still offer a rigid frame or two for the smallest American-made V-Twin, there is nothing like the voluminous selection of accessories—particularly for pre-Evolution Sporties—that exists for Big Twins. This goes a long way toward explaining why so many builders see ratted-out Sportsters as the anti-bling bikes: It's too hard to locate high-end parts, so reflecting your own personality from scratch is often the only path available. But not always. Even the aftermarket is beginning to acknowledge the fascination with old-school customs, as evidenced by the late 2004 release of the retro, small-factory custom Chop-Chop from Kustom Culture Motorcycles. Outfitted to capture the bare bones look of pre-1960s customs while performing with something akin to modern reliability and performance standards, the oddly named Chop-Chop is a study in making the new look genuinely old. A Chopper Guys rigid frame retains a conservative 35-degree stock rake, while KCM has outfitted the machine with a sprung Bates solo seat, medium-high apehanger handlebars, and even a Sportster-style gas tank split down the middle to replicate the look and feel of Indian Motorcycle's old-style split fuel cells.

Bones, a New York City rat rider, revels in the stares and occasional revulsion that his 1967 BSA draws from onlookers.

However, the old timers never enjoyed accessories like a Baker 6-speed transmission with overdrive, an electric starter system (Brando is rolling in his grave!), and a set of modern disc brakes. It's not the first time the manufacturers have addressed what, until recently, had been an underground phenomenon, but a retro bike built to address a retro-retro craze is perhaps a first, even for the chopper movement!

Even some top builders have had some serious fun with the neo-rat bike idea in recent years, including Arlin Fatland of Denver, Colorado's Two Wheelers Motorcycle Shop. In 2002, Fatland, who is better known for full-blown custom bikes smothered in chrome, sporting wide and low front

ends and intricate paint schemes, wowed show judges and audiences by constructing a pair of retro 1950s-era bobbers decked out in flat black livery, detailed with a nifty spider web motif on the stretched Fatbob-style gas tanks and tail-dragger fenders.

Maine's Northeast Chop Shop, a relative new-comer to the chopper game, has also proven fluent in switch-hitting between serious, high-dollar show choppers and neo-rats that maintain the shop's signature, in-your-face, jagged-edged styling.

NCS owner and chief builder Jason Grimes threw a definite curveball to the show crowds in 2005 when he rolled in with a 1950s-style neo-rat chopper that seemed to bear more in common with

The chain brake linkage may have more lash than Estée Lauder, but it sure looks cool!

the custom hot rods of the era than early choppers. The twin, Siamese-style exhaust headers are wrapped in blacked-out fiberglass heat-wrap tape, much like the exhaust systems on early rail dragsters, while Grimes has seen fit to equip each of the pipes with copper end caps for style. Delicate Von Dutch–replica pinstriping adorns the King Sportster gas tank and single fender mounted at the rear. Red powder-coated rims from American Wire Wheel are offset by a high-profile whitewall rear radial tire while the brakeless stock-length springer front end looks like a prop from the art house move classic *The Loveless*.

If it weren't for the late-model Evolution-style engine and rear disc brake, you might think NCS were dealing in genuine retros. "I don't follow a script when I build a chopper or bobber," says Grimes. "I just collect ideas and then start building the parts I think it needs from scratch. I wanted this bike to look like the old 1932 Ford roadsters guys used to make into hot rods back in the day; a really quick no-bullshit bike with as little flash as possible. It was really fun to build because it's not what people expect from us."

In some instances, builders who spend their days struggling to find more impressive and intricate paint jobs and expensive billet aluminum detailing for their show bikes like the idea of building neo-rat choppers. They express an almost childish joy in creating a bike where they can let primer, bare metal, and whatever's left lying around in the parts bin to guide their creative impulses rather than the constant need to out-bling the next guy. As Fatland says, "A simple, uncluttered, and cheap custom bike can be easy to build because you're not sitting around waiting for stuff to come back from the painters and chrome shop. It's what they did back in the 1950s and it really looks cool to see a bike laid out like that again"

Though the trophy show podiums and the parking lots of rallies may still be dominated by chopperdom's other, more affluent side, a few events and rallies have begun to spring up that reflect this burgeoning chopper counterculture, if you will. In Milwaukee, Wisconsin, of all places, the vaunted home of all things Harley and Davidson, a young rider by the name of Scott Radke found himself turned off by what he described as all the "corporate worship and me-too cliquishness" of the orange and black's 100th Anniversary Celebration when 400,000 fans swept through town in 2003.

A frequent visitor to Fuel Café, a hip little coffee shop filled with punkers, hippies, artists, and motorcycle riders of all stripes, Radke got together with Fuel owner Scott Johnson to stage Rockerbox, perhaps the country's only festival embracing the new chopper-custom motorcycle aesthetic. Staged every August, Rockerbox is perhaps the only place where you'll see more flat black paint and hand-stitched saddles than you will triple-dipped show chrome. Chopper builders who know they can't make much of an impression against a six-figure machine at a mainstream

A welder by trade, Bones built his neo-rat with whatever he had lying around the shop, including a fire extinguisher for an oil tank and a battery "box" made from tin and bungee cords. *Mike Seate*

show flock to Rockerbox to be with their own kind, explains Radke, over the roar of several straight-piped choppers, howling four-cylinder streetfighters, and the tinny whine of the occasional Vespa scooter.

What's interesting about events like Rockerbox, besides their ability to bring together all sorts of custom motorcycle enthusiasts, is how the low-buck custom chopper aesthetic manifests itself in so many different forms. There were late-model sportbikes that had been transformed into lowriders, and mid-1970s Harleys made to look like props from Marlon Brando's *The Wild One*. Most used little more than spray paint, hacksaws, and a lot of imagination, which is all Radke says is necessary. "Events like this prove you don't need a million dollars to appreciate custom bikes," he says. "You just need to want to."

Backing that assertion up big-time was an outrageous, low-buck Sporty chopper ridden by Eric Barthule of Kenosha, Wisconsin's K-Town Choppers. The shop is a small, two-man operation involving Eric and brother Jason, and between the two of them they've distilled the essence of a moderately priced chopper down to its bare minimum. Like early chopper builders, they hand-built their own sissy bar, seats, battery box, oil tank, and even the shorty exhaust pipes.

Draped from axle to axle in high-gloss black lacquer, the K-Town bike was graced with a stretched Paughco rigid chassis so low the rider's knuckles could easily scrape the pavement while rounding one of Wisconsin's rare corners. But the K-Town chopper wasn't built for cornering, the owner said. This was an old-school boulevard cruiser, right down to the Hurst jockey shifter, ten-over, Amen springer front end with no brake, and the oversized Fram oil filter hooked to the fender rails. "If you think about what a chopper really needs,

this is about it," beams Barthule. "It has a bored-out motor with Wiseco pistons and an S&S carb so it can really be a handful with just one brake. The original choppers just had a throttle, a tiny little gas tank that held enough fuel to get you back and forth between bars, and someplace to sit. If you wanted to take your girl along, she rolled up a blanket and sat on the fender with her legs across your lap. That's really all you need."

The backstreet rat-chopper movement has also been well represented in the United Kingdom and Europe where many dedicated custom bike fans feel, in no uncertain terms, that there's a certain posh and unmanly air about a high-end chopper. As a result, many of the rank-and-file chopper riders in the United Kingdom rip about on machines that would appear downright ugly at an American bike show. Road grime, instead of being washed away after a ride as we do in the States, is allowed to accumulate as a sort of badge of how many miles the riders have covered. Because many European chopper riders don't own cars or pickup trucks, their machines, ridden in everything from winter sleet to rainy continental springs, tend to look more like the tail end of an 18-wheeler than a pristine piece of two-wheeled jewelry.

This chrome-don't-get-you-home sensibility has become most well-known among American chopper enthusiasts in the spare blacked-out choppers being built by British native Russ Mitchell at Los Angeles' Exile Choppers, though Mitchell's machines only look low-tech. In reality, his neo-rat choppers are every bit as well-constructed, powerful, and exclusive as anything else found above the $50,000 mark.

However, it's the resonance of the less-is-more styling ethos that binds Mitchell's decidedly European approach to choppers to the neo-rat bike to be found in places like the grungy streets of

An antique bottle opener comes in handy for quick beer stops.

New York's Lower East Side. Here, motorcycles need to be stylish for sure, but they also need to be tough enough to do battle with kamikaze taxi cabs, seemingly blind pedestrians, and an environment unfriendly toward chrome and glitz. With a climate subject to its fair share of snow, rain, and smog, many riders argue that the rat bike got its start on the East Coast where chopper riders found it so time-consuming to keep up with polishing their often wet and rusty motorcycles, they simply gave in and let Ma Nature have her way. And plus, it keeps away the thieves, said Bones, a youthful rat-chopper builder and rider we ran into at Sixth Street Specials, a vaunted British bike shop located in an old Latino immigrant neighborhood in New York's East Village.

Bones was typical of the riders who maintained their machines with the assistance of Sixth Street's resident mechanical genius and Scottish expat Hugh Mackie. His motorcycle contained all the clever, imaginative detailing of a far more expensive custom motorcycle—including an antique Pepsi bottle opener mounted on the frame neck, an apparently working-condition fire-extinguisher employed as an oil tank, and an old BSA belt buckle for a brake pedal—but looked about ready to give up the ghost as any minute. Bones, however, says that couldn't be further from the truth. "I get tired of seeing so many choppers in magazines that young guys like me can't afford or are just trailer-queens that don't get dirty because they don't get ridden. I'm a welder by trade, so I just took this old BSA and started chopping it using stuff I found lying around Hugh's shop or stuff I got from my friends," he says.

Even with the solid-mounted solo saddle and 36-inch apehanger handlebars on the 1967 BSA-based chop, Bones has ridden the machine up and down the East Coast as much as 800 miles in a single weekend, proving that rat choppers may look as rough as a New York City garbage truck, but many will run with the best of them.

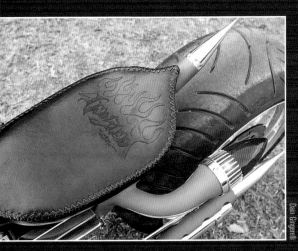

LED SLED

BUILDER: Pat Patterson

ENGINE: 1991 Harley-Davidson XLH
Sportster

DISPLACEMENT: 1,200 cc

EXHAUST: Led Sled Customs

TRANSMISSION: 5-speed with
Jockey Shift

FORKS: Harley-Davidson uppers, Led Sled
piked lowers, 4 inches over

CHASSIS: Led Sled hybrid

DIMENSIONS: 34-degree rake, 8-inch
downtube stretch, 6-inch backbone

SUSPENSION: Kawasaki ZX-11 monoshock

GAS TANK: Led Sled flat-bottom Sportster,
3-gallon

FENDERS: None

SEAT: Black Sheep

SPECIAL FEATURES: Nitrous oxide system
installed

Mike Seate

BARE BONES CUSTOMS

BUILDER: Billy Rogers

ENGINE: 1973 Harley-Davidson

XLCH Sportster

DISPLACEMENT: 1,000 cc

EXHAUST: Homemade shotgun drags

TRANSMISSION: Stock

FORKS: Harley-Davidson, 6 inches over

CHASSIS: Harley-Davidson, with weld-on

hardtail

DIMENSIONS: 38-degree rake

SUSPENSION: None

GAS TANK: Paughco Mustang, 3.8-gallon

FENDERS: (rear) chromed Drag Specialties

SEAT: Ancient white leather solo

Mike Seate

Seate

 Mike Seate

K-TOWN CUSTOMS

BUILDERS: Eric and Jason Barthule

ENGINE: 1980 Harley-Davidson XLH

DISPLACEMENT: 1,000 cc

EXHAUST: Handmade K-Town with fiberglass heat wrap

TRANSMISSION: Stock four-speed with Hurst ratchet shifter

FORKS: Amen springer, 8 inches over

CHASSIS: Paughco hardtail

DIMENSIONS: 40-degree rake, 2 1/4-inch stretch

SUSPENSION: None

GAS TANK: Harley Sportster, 2.25-gallon

FENDERS: K-Town

SEAT: K-Town leather solo

SPECIAL FEATURES: Side-mount automotive oil filter

WHEELS: Spoked, (rear) 18 x 3.5, (front) 21 x 1.75

Dain Gingerelli

KUSTOM CULTURE

BUILDER: Kustom Culture
Motorcycles

ENGINE: Harley-Davidson
Evolution

DISPLACEMENT: 1,340 cc

EXHAUST: KCM

TRANSMISSION: Baker 6-speed

FORKS: Harley-Davidson springer

CHASSIS: Chopper Guys rigid

DIMENSIONS: 35-degree rake,
1 1/2-inch backbone stretch

SUSPENSION: None

GAS TANK: Harley-Davidson
Sportster, split

FENDERS: KCM

SEAT: Bates sprung solo

SPECIAL FEATURES: Electric starter

WHEELS: Harley-Davidson,
(rear) 180 x 18,
(front) 2.25 x 21

Dain Gingerelli

Dain Gingerelli

Simon Green

Simon Green

NORTHEAST CHOP SHOP

BUILDER: Jason Grimes ,

ENGINE: Rev Tech

DISPLACEMENT: 88 cubic inches

EXHAUST: NCS

TRANSMISSION: 4-Speed Rev Tech

FORKS: CCI springer, stock length

CHASSIS: Santee rigid

DIMENSIONS: 33-degree rake,
3-inch downtube stretch

SUSPENSION: Rigid

GAS TANK: 3-gallon King Sportster

FENDERS: NCS

SEAT: NCS solo

WHEELS: American Wire,
(rear) 16 x 140,
(front) 2.25 x 21, powder
coated

Simon Green

chapter 3

FOREIGN BLOOD: IMPORT CHOPPERS MAKE A COMEBACK

It was far from uncommon during the 1970s to see chopped motorcycles rolling down the highways making anything but Harley-Davidson's well-known V-Twin rumble. Even during the dark, technologically crippled days when Milwaukee's most famous motorcycle manufacturer was best known for oil-spewing crankcases and faulty build quality, Hogs were not cheap to own. Many of the choppers Harley-Davidson engines powered were built from the carcasses of former police bikes that had seen years, sometimes decades, of demanding service,

Commonplace on the chopper scene during the 1970s, stretch bikes built from Honda's four-cylinder CB 750 were smooth, adaptable, and quick.

or crash-damaged machines purchased at salvage yards. By contrast, the parallel twin-cylinder motors made by British manufacturers Triumph, Norton, and BSA may not have had much of an edge in the reliability game, but they could be had for a fraction of the price of a domestically produced motor.

In 1969, when Honda first introduced their revolutionary CB 750, not many chopper builders may have taken notice of this futuristic-looking early superbike with its double overhead cams, disc brakes, and odd four-into-four exhaust system. But like all superbikes, from the 40-horsepower Triumph Bonneville of the 1960s to the modern 150-horse Yamaha R-1, many CB 750s were purchased—and subsequently crashed—by riders with more enthusiasm than skill. This left behind a slew of low-mileage motors practically begging for a motorcycle to animate.

It didn't take long before chopper designers saw the potential in Honda's new motor, and for good cause. Its smooth-running four-cylinder powerplant was oil-tight, reliable, and offered none of the paint-shaker vibration of a large-displacement V-Twin. The new Japanese engines were fast, pumping out a good 70 horsepower, a figure only attained by stroking, boring, and radically modifying a Harley-Davidson Big Twin engine. Shoe-horned into a rigid or, later, an early softail-style chassis with plunger suspension, the Honda 750 engine actually looked rather handsome spread across a custom-painted chopper.

This was revolutionary in itself at a time when many hardcore custom bike enthusiasts still incorrectly thought of imported motorcycles as cheap, disposable, and mechanically questionable junk. "Real men ride Harley-powered choppers"

JAN • 72 •

Size was no consideration when assembling an imported chopper in the past. This Honda CB 350 commuter bike receives the full bolt-on custom treatment, right down to its six-bend pullback handlebars and king and queen seat!

was the ethos of the day, a chauvinism backed up by the newly launched custom motorcycle lifestyle magazines that seldom, if ever, published photographs of bikers riding anything but Harley-Davidson choppers. On the streets, of course, the reality was far different. Bikers were eager to get their hands on a chopped motorcycle, and those without the five-figure budgets necessary to afford a domestic chopper made do with whatever they had.

In a matter of less than one year after its introduction, chopper manufacturers at A.E.E., Jammer, and others were offering rigid frame kits, bolt-on hardtail rear ends, and even parts to lower the stock shock absorbers on Honda's biggest production motorbike. By 1971, frames, forks, and complete do-it-yourself chopper kits for a variety of smaller-displacement Hondas were reaching a hungry aftermarket audience.

With the gloves finally off, the import chopper movement was responsible for some wild innovation and, more than occasionally, some downright silly-looking custom motorcycles. As stretched and raked frames became available for smaller-displacement bikes such as Honda's CB 350 twin and 550-Four, the tiny engines often looked like lawn-mower motors when planted inside such lengthy chassis. Likewise, many builders took a shortcut to chopping metric bikes, simply installing a set of inappropriately long fork tubes or a cheaply made king and queen seat and a sloppily attached Mustang or peanut gas tank with airbrushed murals for some eye-charring results.

Nevertheless, the explosion of the imported chopper market once and for all erased the previously held belief that custom motorcycles had to be made from American source materials and in years to come, its enduring popularity would help spur the Japanese manufacturers to produce their own lines of "Specials," "Low-Slingers,"and other factory customs to mixed success.

Though they sold in respectable enough numbers over the past 20 years, the Japanese cruisers were often an odd interpretation of what choppers were really about. At first, the Japanese can be said to have gotten the basic formula wrong. In many cases, as with Yamaha's XS11, or Kawasaki's mercifully short-lived KZ750 LTD, engines from standards and sportbikes were simply re-assigned to cruiser duty. The gas tanks were pressed on an assembly line with slightly more of a teardrop shape; seats received a little extra foam padding and a raised passenger pad; and fenders, for some inexplicable reason, were chromed. Handlebars were bolted on in an unusual variety of bands and pull-back shapes, clearly mimicking the chopper styling seen on the streets, but the Japanese did so with one foot kept conservatively on the floor—the paint schemes were as bland as Irish oatmeal and nobody seemed to bother re-designing the megaphone exhaust pipes lifted directly from sportbikes. Mostly ridiculed in custom magazines with tags such as "cross-dressers" and "Yama-Harleys" it would be another 10 years before Honda's graceful American Classic Edition would break the plasticky Japanese cruiser mold.

Meanwhile, 30 years after chopper builders first saw the customizing potential in Honda's early four-cylinder streetbikes, the same factors that drove them to seek alternative powerplants still exist. Some motorcycle enthusiasts find the overwhelming popularity of Harley-Davidson motors among chopper builders to be enough of a turn-off to send them seeking alternative power sources. While The Motor Company is famously litigious in some matters (attempting, unsuccessfully,

to patent the fabled potato-potato sound of its single crank-pin V-Twins, for instance), they have been more lenient when it comes to the aftermarket. As a result, countless parts manufacturers have flooded the market with imitation Harley-Davidson engine components and even entire motors. Custom builders can pick from their choice of mock-Harley engines in every conceivable displacement configuration while some firms like Alabama's Accurate Engineering have even introduced a line of replica vintage engines built to resemble Harley's vaunted Panheads, Knuckleheads and Shovelheads.

Add to this already impressive roster dozens of what are known as turn-key chopper manufacturers who produce thousands of machines all running big-bore V-Twins modeled on various Milwaukee designs. In such a single-minded marketplace, it almost makes a statement of sorts to choose an imported engine for a project bike, just as it did more than three decades ago. Surprisingly, many of these left-leaning builders choose to build their machines around vintage Triumph and Honda CB 750 engines. This is mostly due to the advent of water-cooling systems on most large-displacement imported motorcycles. With the boxy radiators, voluminous cooling hoses, fans, and exposed plumbing on these high-tech engines, they're less aesthetically pleasing to the eye than the simple uncluttered lines of an air-cooled motor and, therefore, less likely to find themselves bolted into a custom chassis.

"I looked around and saw that just about every chopper for sale or every chopper built by the big shops had a Harley or Harley-clone motor in it and I just wanted to do something different," says Dave Woeful of Holstein, Wisconsin, about his motivation for building his dream machine from a 1973 Honda CB 750 engine.

Dropped shocks, a raked-out stock chassis, and a set of eight-over forks make this low-buck Honda chopper a winner—and for about one-eighth the cost of a domestic chopper of the same caliber.

 Mike Seate

At first glance, the gold and red stretch chop looks like something that just rolled in from the parking lot of an Allman Brothers concert, circa 1975. It sports a set of chromed five-spoke Invader mag wheels, a popular accessory item from the days of peace signs and VW busses, plus a set of chromed girder forks 8 inches longer than stock. The bodywork is also of a 1970s vintage, the angular, hexagonal gas tank sorting a massive chrome nameplate with a Honda logo etched in for extra dazzle. Bikes like this are becoming so popular that an owner's club has been launched in the Midwest—the Honda Multi Club (www.cb750.org) to help the faithful network, track down parts, and generally share their infatuation with the early superbike.

Woeful is as proud of his self-built retro chopper as any customer riding around town on a hand-built chopper from Bourget's or Billy Lane; that it cost less than $10,000 to complete, right down to the chromed bicycle squeeze horn mounted on the left engine head, makes the project that much more unique. "I could have spent ten grand and just ended up with a Harley-Davidson engine and had to keep saving money and buying parts from there," says Woeful. "But when I park this Honda somewhere, I'm always surprised by how many guys come up to me and start telling me about the weird imported choppers they built back in the day. There was a lot more of these on the road than people think."

This rider may hail from Harley-Davidson's hometown of Milwaukee, Wisconsin, but his chopper runs on Honda CB 550 power; the peanut gas tank is American-made.

Woeful's observation is borne out by the sheer volume of old-school import chopper parts that can still be found on the market. Admittedly, it takes a resourceful mind and a considerable bit of digging, but everything from twisted-rail springer forks, bobtail fenders, sissy bars, and chassis are still out there. Swap meets, small custom parts emporiums, and the ever-helpful Internet auction house eBay are all good sources for tracking down imported chopper components, as are European websites specializing in alternative custom ideas.

As in the 1970s, a number of builders are starting to employ ever-diverse powerplants to their choppers, to sometimes bizarre, but always interesting, effect. Using a mixture of Harley-Davidson aftermarket parts, stock Yamaha components, and hand-built custom accessories, Dane Regis of Chicago built an impressive hardtail chopper from a Yamaha XS 650 twin. Regis says the machine gives up nothing in horsepower or torque to, say, a Harley Sportster powerplant, and the self-taught chopper builder is proud of having the resourcefulness to complete a

chopper project from such an unlikely motorcycle. Long considered the engine that Triumph should have manufactured had they wanted to remain in business during the 1980s, the horizontally opposed twin has reappeared in recent years as a customized, flat track racer and as a stripped-down café racer, testament to its unprecedented 14-year production run which ended in 1983.

Likewise, Kawasaki's massively powerful Z-1 engines are again being used to power choppers and custom lowriders, just as they had during the last custom motorcycle craze. Many builders joke that it's less sacrilegious to bolt a four-cylinder big Kaw motor into a stretched, low-slung frame than it would be to vulcanize, say, a sweet-handling Ducati motor for a chopper because the stock Kawasaki chassis was never able to properly contain the engine's whopping powerband in the first place! Not as many of these in-line fours are being built anew as when the Z-1's reign ended in the early 1980s, when the aforementioned water-cooling era began in earnest for the Japanese superbike manufacturers.

Still, the development of water-cooling systems hasn't completely swayed chopper builders from embracing them, particularly among European custom bike fans who seem to feel that anything this side of a one-man rickshaw can be used to power a chopper. Flip through the glossy pages of magazines such as England's *Back Street Heroes* or Ireland's grubby *100 Percent Biker* and there appears to be an ongoing shop-class project in place that rewards the builder who can fabricate a chopper out of the most unlikely of sources. The inevitable rat's nest of electrical wiring and coolant tubing surrounding modern water-cooled engines is no deterrent to the foreign chopper builders who've made a genuine folk art out of adapting—or could that be "adopting"—rare machinery for choppers. Over here, custom motorcycle shows will bring out a mind-blowing assortment of machines most American builders would never even imagine putting near a welding torch; chopped Honda Gold Wing touring bikes are not uncommon, replete with homemade springer and girder forks.

Nik Samson, former editor for England's *Streetfighter* magazine, explained how British custom bike builders, whether they choose streetfighters or choppers, are more interested in outright performance than many American builders. The European riders' dedication to high-performance riding—and a limited budget, in many cases—has resulted in Old Country chopper builders eagerly grabbing the fastest, most powerful engines on the market for their project bikes, regardless of country of origin while, in more recent years, Scandinavian builders (which we'll see more

A blacked-out bobber made from a mid-1980s Kawasaki KZ-750 LTD. The lack of a rear fender means this rider is going home alone!

This rider blends nationalities on his retro Triumph chopper with a set of 3.5-gallon Fatbob gas tanks from a Harley.

of in the next chapter) have even started chopping up late-model metric cruisers from Suzuki, Yamaha, Kawasaki, and Honda for radical project bikes.

Because modern motorcycles tend to be far more technologically complex than their forbearers in the 1970s—consider the complex exhaust and air box designs needed to meet world pollution emissions standards, or the array of electrics and computer circuitry required for engine management and fuel injection—it is, mechanically speaking, far more difficult to build a chopper from, say, a Kawasaki Vulcan 1600 than it was to simply yank the engine from a Yamaha XS 650 and bolt it into an aftermarket frame. Even upgrading a stock

chassis with enough custom bolt-ons to make it appear unique is no easy task for builders working with modern metric cruisers as their chunky frames, shaft drive systems, and relatively small number of firms building custom parts for these bikes make for tough going.

Fortunately, Yamaha introduced a motorcycle in 1999 that began to change all that. The XV 1600, or Road Star, with its pushrod-operated valves on a Harley-Davidson Shovelhead look-alike engine and softail-style rear suspension, came about only after Harley-Davidson appeared to have backed off trying to patent its designs in the courts. With no further threats from the lawyers in

Though the air-cooled, parallel twin engine propelling this groovy little retro chopper was last produced in 1982, Triumph continues to represent in the modern import chopper scene. *Mike Seate*

Milwaukee, it allowed a Japanese manufacturer to, for perhaps the first time, create an engine design that was simple and uncluttered enough in appearance and traditional enough in function that it would lend itself rather well to custom chopper projects. Yamaha's clever marketing department was well aware that the Japanese cruiser bikes had failed to inspire American custom builders the way they had originally hoped. With Harley-Davidson taking an increasingly larger slice of the large-displacement motorcycle market

for each of the past nine years in the United States, and fostering a burgeoning parts aftermarket worth billions, the big four Japanese manufacturers worked feverishly to create new cruisers that would lend themselves to custom projects and owner upgrades.

When the first XV 1600 was revealed at the International Motorcycle Shows in 1999, it shared floor space with another XV, this one given the full-custom treatment by metric aftermarket powerhouse Cobra. It was a glimpse into the future, one

The builder of this Triumph chopper was clearly obsessed with early 1960s detailing, right down to the metalflake riding helmet and whitewall tire on a narrow 18-inch spoked rim.

where, at least overseas, the dominance of the Harley-Davidson engine would face its first real competition in the custom motorcycle market. Already in place were several top-flight aftermarket parts suppliers such as exhaust experts Vance and Hines, Jardine, Mustang Seats, and Kuryakyn supplying a number of bolt-on accessories for metric cruiser enthusiasts.

However, it was in Germany where the veritable explosion of metric choppers really began to take form. One of the most impressive manufacturers for aftermarket metric choppers and chopper parts is undoubtedly Hamminkeln, Germany's Thunderbike, that produced custom parts for dozens of late-model Japanese cruisers. Taking the challenges of creating custom parts for metric choppers head-on, Thunderbike has crafted everything from custom exhaust systems to shock-lowering kits, trick fenders, and even billet aluminum wheels for these sometimes neglected machines.

Perhaps their most ambitious work went into the stunning "Dragster" and "Gothik" chopper kits for Yamaha's XV1600. Built with typical German precision and detailed with the sort of visual flair usually associated with $100,000 show bikes, the Thunderbike kits take the lead provided by A.E.E. and Jammer to an entirely different level. The Dragster kit employs a clever hidden suspension system and a gull-shaped swingarm; up front, in respect to Germany's famously restrictive vehicle design laws, a set of V-Tech stock-length upside-down forks appear much longer than they are due to a lazy 40-degree rake. The chassis is made from thick-diameter 1-1/4 cold rolled steel and can run either the XV's stock monoshock rear suspension or a special Thunderbike air ride unit and tires up to a walloping 300 millimeters in width. Because Yamaha designed the XV 1600 to run a carbureted engine rather than employing a fuel-injection system, Thunderbike was able to create a series of head-turning air cleaners and exhaust systems for the big bike.

Thumbing through their voluminous Custom Book catalogs, it's hard to tell you're not looking at a Harley-Davidson aftermarket catalog. Yamaha Motor Corporation has long worked in conjunction with American aftermarket houses, assisting them in developing exhaust systems and other parts for its new cruisers, but in Thunderbike's catalogs, you'll find a first, complete XV1600 engines for sale to custom builders, a move that signals the Japanese might finally be putting the full weight of their corporate know-how behind the metric chopper movement.

Back home in the United States, the radical customizing of late-model imported bikes is only now getting underway. With Harley-Davidson now controlling the lion's share of the large-displacement motorcycle market, it's hard to imagine the streets filling up with radically chopped late-model Yamahas and Kawasakis anytime soon. But still, the formidable task of turning modern imported iron into choppers does have its fans. Pat Patterson of Ohio's Led Sled Customs has recently completed a funky, blacked-out chopper from the remains of a Triumph Daytona supersport bike, building a one-off frame for the three-cylinder, water-cooled powerplant with a custom chassis-making jig that Patterson designed himself.

Encouraged by the reaction to the bike, which looks like a prop from the Mel Gibson film *The Road Warrior*, Patterson encourages customers to bring him even weirder motors for his future chopper projects. "If you have a frame jig that allows you to build the frame around the engine, there's really no limit to what kind of engine you can build a chopper around," says Patterson. "A lot of guys think radiators and wiring is a problem, but if you're into using your imagination, they can become part of the real raw, industrial look of a motorcycle."

As with all custom chopper projects built from scratch, it takes a considerable amount of work to create a running, functioning motorcycle from just a chassis and engine. Bikes such as Triumph's 120-horsepower Daytona were designed to run smoothly with purpose-built exhaust systems built to work with the stock air box. Removing the pipes means hand-bending a three-into-one system that will still allow the big Triumph to run properly and look good at the same time. Still, Patterson loves the challenge of making a chopper from unlikely sources. "Anybody can plunk down the money for a big-money expensive designer chopper. And don't get me wrong, I love those bikes. But I'd rather do something that nobody else has done before," he says.

iN EUROPE, THEY'LL CHOP ANYTHiNG

Visit any of the major European chopper rallies and you'll notice something odd: the number of custom bikes in attendance will rival, if not surpass, anything you'll see at American biker gatherings from Sturgis to Daytona, but the ubiquitous rumble and roar of the vaunted Harley-Davidson V-Twin engine is only one of the sounds you'll hear. Instead, the European builders—whether we're talking high-profile custom legends such as Sweden's Tolle Denisch or England's Projex custom works—regard the utilization of foreign powerplants as a time-honored practice.

Much of this can be attributed to the long history the European riding community has with Japanese motorcycles. When Triumph, Norton, and the other main British motorcycle manufacturers went under in the 1960s and 1970s, many riders—including chopper builders—wasted little time adapting to the influx of high-performance bikes offered by the Japanese. The new generation of in-line, four-cylinder bikes rolling out of the Far East proved to be everything the British parallel twins were not: fast, reliable, and, for some uncanny reason, capable of keeping their lubricating fluids inside their crankcases instead of all over the car park.

Even though there were few parts available for a European custom builder to transform his Kawasaki Z-1 or Yamaha XS-11 into a raked-out chopper, it didn't stop the crafty Euro

riders from building one-off frames for their beloved Japanese motors. And why not?! Harley-Davidson's motorcycles have always been considered prohibitively expensive for European riders due to import fees and taxes.

Mike Seate

This outlaw club rolled into a rally at England's Brighton Pier on choppers powered by an odd selection of engines, including a three-cylinder Yamaha 850 from the 1980s and a Honda CB-1100F Supersport powerplant.

The tradition in motorcycling in the States has always been laid-back low-speed cruising, whereas the Europeans have a nearly religious affection for speed, even among chopper riders. And without the rabid patriotism that permeates the U.S. custom bike scene, there was really no spiritual reason to build a chopper out of an American-made motorcycle.

As a result, many overseas chopper builders relished the challenge of turning a sharp-handling, futuristic-looking, sport-oriented Japanese motorcycle into something that practically slinked down the boulevard like a chrome and lacquered python. With a deep appreciation for metal working emphasized in technical and secondary schools in Germany and the Scandinavian countries, it wasn't unusual to find young men leaving school already possessing the skills needed to weld steel tubing into a rigid motorcycle chassis or cut and extend the rake dimensions on a stock Suzuki frame to make it look like something they'd seen in those funky American motorcycle magazines.

The Japanese bikes also came with some added amenities that lent themselves perfectly to the low-buck European chopper movement: the disc brakes and wire wheels offered strong stopping capabilities. The solid-state Japanese electrics could be conveniently hidden away in small, chromed circuit boxes that were bolted to frames and machining a set of extended tubes, for a stock set of O.E.M. forks ensured a builder could maintain the quality and control of stock equipment while still looking the business. Because an in-line, four-cylinder engine vibrated far less than a large-capacity V-Twin, an imported chopper seldom suffered from

the harmonic parts-shedding that affects so many rigid-mounted Harley choppers, not to mention being kinder to fragile electrical components that always seem to commit suicide while riding home in the dark.

Today, with the runaway popularity of the American chopper movement, there are quite a few more Harley-Davidson–powered choppers profiling down European roads, many of which are capable of giving an Eddie Trotta or Cyril Huze bike a run for its creative money. They're still far more expensive and rare than they are back home, but there's a status and authenticity to riding American iron for a European rider that's attracting an increasing number of new owners each year.

However, the appreciation for the smoothness of an in-line, four-cylinder motor bolted into a low-slung chopper frame is a tradition that continues unabated in the foreign market. The undeniably strong sense of British pride has lured dozens of builders to create custom sleds around the new water-cooled Triumph three-cylinder motors, which is quite a formidable challenge given the elaborate water-cooling systems on these sturdy machines. And, just as they did in the 1970s, European builders are still almost possessed when it comes to adopting the latest, fastest Japanese sportbike engines for custom applications, with everything from Yamaha's blistering 155-horsepower YZFR-1 and Honda's torque-monster 1,800-cc VTX motor. It's unproven whether the foreign chopper will ever establish as much of a presence in the domestic market as it has overseas, but the variety the Euro choppers present is a wonderful example of the old adage that a lack of funds can't stop a creative mind from making memorable art.

Mike Seate

Mike Seate

Mike Seate

DAVE WOEFUL

BUILDER: Dave Woeful

ENGINE: Honda CB 750

DISPLACEMENT: 750 cc

EXHAUST: Drag pipes

TRANSMISSION: Stock

FORKS: Girder, 10 inches over

CHASSIS: A.E.E. swingarm

DIMENSIONS: 40-degree rake,
6-inch stretch

SUSPENSION: Drag Specialties

GAS TANK: A.E.E., hex-shaped

FENDERS: A.E.E.

SEAT: Drag Specialties

SPECIAL FEATURES: Chrome work
and custom paint by owner,
air horn

WHEELS: Invader Mags,
(rear) 18 inches,
(front) 21 inches

DRAGSTER

THUNDERBIKE

BUILDER: Thunderbike
of Germany

ENGINE: Yamaha XV1600

DISPLACEMENT: 1,600 cc

EXHAUST: Thunderbike drag pipes

TRANSMISSION: Stock 5-speed

FORKS: V-Tech

CHASSIS: Thunderbike

DIMENSIONS: 40-degree rake

SUSPENSION: Air-ride

GAS TANK: Thunderbike, 4-gallon

FENDERS: Thunderbike

SEAT: Thunderbike

SPECIAL FEATURES: Can run wide
tires, fully road-legal

WHEELS: Thunderbike 3-D billet

Mike Seate

Mike Seate

DANE REGIS

BUILDER: Dane Regis

ENGINE: Yamaha

DISPLACEMENT: 650 cc

EXHAUST: Owner, hand-bent

TRANSMISSION: Stock 5-speed

FORKS: Yamaha, 6 inches over

CHASSIS: Jammer hardtail

DIMENSIONS: 38-degree rake,
4-inch stretch

SUSPENSION: None

GAS TANK: 3.5-gallon, Mustang

FENDERS: Flat steel

SEAT: Drag Specialties

SPECIAL FEATURES: Downdraft
air cleaners, homemade
forward controls

WHEELS: Yamaha spoked, 18
inches rear, 19 inches front

Mike Seate

69

chapter 4

MASTER CLASS: EXPERTISE & EXCELLENCE

MILWAUKEE IRON

Imagine spending half your life designing custom motorcycles. You start off in a small garage owned by a friend, or wrenching and welding custom parts in some dingy unlit corner of a pal's basement, investing untold hours in a craft you've perfected just because it's a lot of fun. You build a sissy bar or a gas tank and a set of fenders for a friend and he loves it. You sit back and bask in pride each time he rides by, and soon, word of mouth spreads and you're doing the same for his friends, and then their friends, and on it goes. You keep at it through marriage, raising children, and more man-hours than you really care to remember.

This bike was built by Milwaukee Iron, the shop featured on the popular TV show *Southern Steel.*

And then one day, you discover that you've suddenly got the skills and wherewithal to construct an entire custom motorcycle from scratch, a machine that will display all your talents and techniques simultaneously, showing the world that 'you have the skills to pay the bills and then some. You bust your knuckles and burn your jeans and empty your family's bank account one thousand times making that vision in your head into an actual running motorcycle. You even manage to piss off a few folks along the way with your single-minded determination, while your credit card statements are starting to contain more zeroes than a Milwaukee Brewers scorecard.

Ah, but then one day it happens. Your custom bike becomes so popular and wins so many show trophies, you begin another, and then another. By the end of a year, you've rented out a small retail space, hired on a couple of friends to help with the painting and parts orders and the phone that never seems to cease ringing. Your shop's walls soon become plastered with pages from magazine

Blending 1960s, 1970s, and twenty-first-century style, Milwaukee Iron follows no one.

articles written about your custom bikes and, hey, wasn't that just some guy from a cable TV station calling to shoot an episode at your shop?

It's a rare story, but by now one that should ring familiar with more than a few of the world's top-flight chopper mechanics. Talk with the folks at the top of their game, the fabricators and wizards with a welding torch and the visionaries who've spent half a lifetime bent over a drafting table and a shop lift bench, and they'll typically express genuine surprise, even shock, that the world is suddenly beating a path to their door. Guys who, a generation before, might have hoped for a day gig stripping down police bikes at their local Harley-Davidson

dealership are now buying beach homes in Florida, traveling to industry shows in Europe, feted by journalists, and filling the pages of custom aftermarket catalogs with billions of dollars worth of handmade motorcycle parts.

But heavy is the head that wears the crown, as they say. Being on top of the chopper game only means there's always some young half-broke, but damn determined, upstart breathing down your welder's apron, somebody who wants what you have more than you ever did. 'You have player haters making T-shirts dissing your name and asking "Jesse Who?" and declaring on bumper stickers how they don't give a damn how they do it in your neck of the woods. There's entire Internet discussion boards filled with wannabes with nothing better to do than endlessly analyze and dissect your every move. 'You even have to deal with European chopper artists weaned on high-tech and wildly accurate computer-aided drafting equipment, insurance companies who refuse to insure your work for the road, and the uneasy recurring feeling that someday this could all fall flat and you'll be back in your riding buddy's 10 x 12 garage, hammering out fender blanks for a handshake, $50, and a cold beer.

Maybe, says Randy Simpson of Lynchburg, Virginia's Milwaukee Iron, but it's been one hell of a ride, from welding steel duct work for hospital ventilation systems to starring in his own chopper-building weekly show on cable television's Discovery Channel. Simpson was busier than the proverbial one-legged man in the ass-kicking contest when he stilled himself for a spell and explained how much he loved his work, despite the pitfalls, the missed deadlines, and the pressures of being a celebrity chopper builder. In a soft, southern drawl, Simpson, 47, confessed that he never anticipated doing anything more with his love of motorcycles and his considerable metalworking skills than to maybe build a few parts to help other antique motorcycle enthusiasts rebuild and maintain their rides.

His shop's name, Milwaukee Iron, was chosen in 1983 as a plain-spoken tribute to his intent. The first dozen years in business were spent mostly performing mundane repairs and restoration work on antique Harleys—case repairs, transmission rebuilds, and more—in a cluttered smoky workshop arranged in his mother' basement. However, Simpson had experience operating all sorts of machinery, from lathes to band saws, English wheels, and anything else necessary to turn flat sheet steel into motorcycle parts. With a set of old chassis jigs from the Harley-Davidson factory, Simpson was able to offer frame-straightening and repair work on chassis dating back to the 1930s, a period he reveres as the pinnacle of design for the Motor Company.

"I was always working on other people's bikes, but along the way I'd devised all sorts of things to make them better. We had the idea for the first triple trees with internal fork stops, and I'd made lots of steel fenders even back when people were saying that fiberglass fenders were the next big thing," says Simpson. "I built a custom bike from the ground up that was dedicated to the band Lynyrd Skynyrd, and it ended up winning the Rat's Hole Custom show at Daytona that year."

Groundbreaking for its use of a vented primary cover, a flush-mount pop-up gas cap, and strutless rear fender, the bike proved a true crowd pleaser. And, as often happens, Simpson soon found his phone wouldn't stop ringing, with customers demanding their own custom bikes done up in his inimitable style. Over the next two decades, the shop played with its love of early American motorcycle designs and choppers, building parts that would trick out a stock machine while still, miraculously, paying homage to the purpose-built board track racers and drag bikes that spawned the chopper movement.

Though the antique replacement parts, business at Milwaukee Iron often grew so large that Simpson was unable to find the time to pursue the custom chopper bug, he received inspiration for a custom ride in the late 1990s that turned his wheels permanently back in the direction of full fabrication. Simpson's retro racer, dubbed Old Yeller, was a wicked exercise in period customization, combining a late-model engine with a multiple-loop rigid frame that, to the untrained eye, looked like it had been yanked out from under a 1930s Harley-Davidson race bike. With a narrow-glide springer front end, a mockup of one of Harley's old rectangular gas tanks, and more detailing than a Pieter Bruegel painting, the machine sent Milwaukee Iron's custom ideas back into the spotlight.

From there, Simpson's 14-person crew never looked back. The time was right for building far-out one-of-a-kind custom choppers, and the shop now splits its duties equally between this and the manufacture of antique replacement parts. They've upgraded their equipment to suit, employing a 3,500-watt laser to cut steel blanks into the basic shapes for fenders; and frames can now be rigged together thanks to a series of custom frame jigs. It makes for a hectic unforgiving workday, Simpson admits, but the rewards have been amazing to say the least. "I sometimes shake my head and can't believe I'm really getting paid to do something I love. I must be the luckiest S.O.B. on the planet," he says with a laugh.

Lucky, yes, but there's been plenty of hard work along the way. The purple chopper with the tall organ exhaust pipes that Milwaukee Iron built actually came together in just 15 manic days of build time, a challenge the shop's crew accepted only after the proposition was floated by a Discovery Channel film crew. The bike's construction was used for the pilot episode of the show *Southern Chopper* and utilizes many of the techniques Simpson and crew devised while rebuilding antique bikes over the years. The frame is equipped with a unique arched support brace above the engine compartment, a strengthening apparatus that makes the chassis more rigid, and evokes the look of his beloved 1930s Harley-Davidson race bikes.

With a typical build time on an MI chopper closer to six months than 15 days, Simpson said the

experience taught him the importance of being well-organized—even if the TV show tended to overstate any problems or mistakes the crew made during construction.

"Building a bike that fast from the ground up, you realize you really have to have all your ducks in a row. We'd met the camera crew well ahead of time and my guys all got along with them and didn't mind them being here, so it all went well. But if people think that a shop can really rush through building a chopper if they don't have all the right equipment and a good, dedicated, and experienced staff, they're in for a surprise," he says.

Whether the chopper craze sustains momentum for another five years is anyone's guess, Simpson says, but he's glad to have gotten himself in on the ground floor when it all hit. "There's no way I could have predicted this back in 1983. Back then, Harley-Davidson dealerships were going bankrupt and, like a dummy, I had this great idea to start a motorcycle dealership at the same time! We spent years building custom bikes out of broken, used and busted-up parts, stuff that needed repairs just to put it back on the road," says Simpson. "It's just amazing that we're doing all these full-on custom show bikes today and people love them. It's just amazing."

LOGIC CHOPPERS

Over in the quiet, pastoral farmland of Ohio's Amish country, Rick Hoffman also got his start building amazing custom motorcycles during the less-then-glamorous custom bike scene of the early 1980s. The burly, bearded Hoffman remembers a time when police officers routinely pulled over custom choppers for roadside inspections, and grizzled outlaws were riding most of the stretch bikes on the road. In contrast, when we caught up

This orange softail built by Rick Hoffman of Logic Choppers is comfortable and cool.

with Hoffman in the Salem, Ohio, workshop and headquarters for his curiously named Logic Motorcycle Company, he was preparing a newly built softail sled for a customer who was flying in on his private Lear jet for a test ride.

"The clientele has definitely changed, and the people who buy my choppers sometimes haven't ever ridden a motorcycle, or it's been ten, twenty years since they threw a leg over a saddle. It's a lot for them to be getting into, but we try and make the transition as easy as possible," says Hoffman, 'whose bald head and long red beard have been made famous in a series of high-profile ads for the Geico insurance underwriting firm.

In a true sign of the times, much of Hoffman's business involves arranging full insurance coverage for his customers, as underwriting a chopper to protect it against theft (a frequent problem), accidents, or mechanical mishaps can be a major stumbling block to ownership. Worse yet, many banks and lending institutions flatly refuse to provide financing for custom-built motorcycles, which are of unknown manufacturing origin.

At Logic, which Hoffman launched in early 2003 after losing most of his equipment, tooling, and parts stock in a fire, Hoffman is making the transition from TV chopper fan to highway rider much easier. He's been experimenting with a centrifugal clutch mechanism, which alleviates the pants-wetting danger new riders face when stopping and starting a motorcycle with a massive engine and long wheelbase on a hill. He's also earned a full manufacturer's license, which means banks and insurance companies recognize

Logic as a reputable motorcycle builder, complete with a nationwide dealer network and full financing.

"If we can take most of the human error out of riding a chopper, the insurance companies will love you. I meet guys all the time who want to buy choppers but they can't get them insured because nobody knows what they're worth," says Hoffman, who even has Logic's half-dozen models listed in the Kelly Blue Book of vehicle appraisals.

Hoffman had actually given up the custom bike biz after the devastating fire at his old shop, but he said after a year off he really couldn't deal with the loss of his main creative outlet. As a member of the famous Hamsters Motorcycle Club, a collection of respected custom builders and chopper enthusiasts known for their bright yellow T-shirts and equally eye-popping bikes, Hoffman said he was deluged with calls to fabricate bikes for friends. "This time, I decided to do it the right way," he said.

The new shop was opened at the Quaker City Dragway, a quarter-mile strip located in southeastern Ohio. With the strip at his disposal for testing and tuning purposed, Hoffman also uses the strip to give customers test rides on their new machines. He chose the name Logic and the slogan "Think About It" for the chopper line, in deference to his lifetime interest in philosophy and intellectual pursuits. The first series of bikes were to be named after his heroes, including Socrates and the Austrian physicist Albert Einstein. However, legal problems and trademark issues arose from using the Einstein name, so Hoffman instead titled his choppers after obscure religions, dinosaurs, and various anthropological oddities.

The Logic line is designed to incorporate all the flash and floss style that makes choppers so popular with riders and non-riders alike, but the rake and trail dimensions are under careful study to make sure the sensation of piloting one of these 700-pound, 100-plus horsepower beasts isn't scary or wild for new riders. The Raptor, a sinewy, pavement-scraping cross between a pro-street drag bike and a digger-style Bay Area chopper, is among the most popular model of the 200 bikes Logic produces each year, and is by far the easiest to ride. Decked out with Wicked Brothers' Undertaker swept-back exhaust pipes, pull-back one-piece handlebars, and a stretched gas tank covered in sliver metalflake tribal graphics, the bike has a certain sophisticated charm about it not unlike a BMW sportscar.

The whopping 240-mm rear tire is a detail that, Hoffman says, his customers wouldn't do without. "Fat tires are the new craze, like the extended front ends of the 1970s. Most people don't care that a tire, once it gets over 280 millimeters or so, will really affect a bike's handling in a bad way. When the rear tire is that much wider than the front, when you go to turn a corner, the bike will just fight you all the way because they don't want to track straight. And now they're coming out with a 360, which is just insane. But people really like the looks," he said.

The firm's orange stretch chopper, dubbed the Voodoo, is a cool kicked-back chopper in classic California style, fronted by a set of inverted forks with a full 12 inches of extension, a 110-cubic-inch fully polished motor from Korea's Rev Tech and, in deference to the advanced age of many custom chopper riders these days, a full air-ride suspension system located beneath the 5.5-inch rear rim. 'Hoffman is soon to introduce a new line of Logic choppers labeled Black Pearl, which will be an extreme high-end line of bikes, replete with LED lighting frenched into the fenders, custom-made frames, and fully polished 124-cubic-inch high-performance motors from legendary tuner Kendall Johnson.

Hoffman insists that customers visit the shop, if possible, where he can adjust the handlebars, forward controls, and other amenities to suit their bodies and particular riding style. And if they're not interested in a run down Quaker City's quarter-mile, there's plenty of cue ball–smooth back roads to test out their new wheels.

With a manufacturer's license to his credit, Hoffman must invest more than the average amount of R&D work into his choppers, which are covered by a full manufacturer's warranty should anything shake loose out on the road. He's had one of his coal black-and-orange flamed Headhunter choppers up to somewhere around 135 miles per hour at the strip during a test, which should be enough for most customers. Logic also performs several weeks of endurance testing on its machines, with *American Riders* magazine journalist Chris Maida clocking an impressive 2,500 miles on one of Hoffman's bikes for a recent article. "I'd done an experimental build using a new motor from S&S, and all we had during the entire test ride was a failed stator and one of the handlebar bolts coming loose while he was sitting still in a parking lot. It had a 12-over springer front end but it was built so well, he could still ride it around in a tight circle in a parking lot with one hand. These bikes are definitely well-balanced," Hoffman says proudly.

Though Hoffman's typical customer has changed over the past two decades, he says the strangest part of being a chopper builder, at a time when the machines are at their pop culture zenith, is what people expect from him. "The whole TV thing has actually made it harder to do my job than it used to be," he explains. "Sure, there's more business, but they think you can build them a motorcycle to their exact specifications in just two days like they do on TV and I tell them it's just not possible." In the future, Hoffman expects chopper riders to

Simon Green

Never afraid to experiment, Dave Perewitz completed this wild underslung Sportster in the mid-1970s.

take a pass on the radically stretched bikes and opt for the pro-street look, which he says are easier to ride long distances. But in the meantime, he'll keep steady building both kinds. It's only logical.

CYCLE FAB-ULOUS

Though Massachusetts' Dave Perewitz appears to lead one crazy high-octane lifestyle, the legendary northeast chopper guru actually prefers the quiet life. His shop, Cycle Fabrications in Bridgewater, Massachusetts, is a hubbub of activity, with showers of sparks from welder's torches, constantly ringing telephones, and, more recently, camera crews from cable TV parked in his office. But Perewitz, who has undeniably led the region in custom motorcycle innovation over the past 30 years, prefers life at his family's comfortable country house, where the only sounds are the rustling of leaves in the trees. Well, that and the roar of a Perewitz custom chopper being fired to life for one of his frequent rides.

After 30 years in the business, a Perewitz bike is as easily recognizable as, say, a custom concept car by George Barris. The intricately designed paint and graphics, the monochrome forks and detailing, and the less-is-more approach to chopper building have brought the Brockton, Massachusetts, native hoards of celebrity customers and the sort of fame usually reserved for sports heroes and film stars. But even in the age of oversized media exposure for custom motorcycle builders and the equally oversized egos that too often accompany it, Perewitz is still largely unaffected by stardom. His frequent appearances on the Discovery Channel's *Great Biker Build-Off* series have allowed him a certain amount of creative freedom, he says; meaning he doesn't have to pass his ideas through a planning committee like many builders do to attract customers. Most of his bikes have standing offers for purchase before he's even finished building them, he says.

"I like to take 'em out and wring them out on the roads a little before I sell them. And some of the bikes, you take so much time going over every last little detail that you kind of don't want to sell; but rule number one is you can never, ever get attached to them. So once a project is finished, I feel like I've overcome that challenge and I sell them so I can get on to the next one," he says.

By constantly challenging himself to create ever-more appealing and technologically complex custom motorcycles, Perewitz—who built his first custom Harley Sportster in 1971 to ride to the nearby Weirs Beach Rally at Laconia, New Hampshire—has amassed a client list that includes NASCAR CEO Mike Helton, Aerosmith guitarist Brad Whitford, and several NFL all-stars. In 2003, Dave received one of the biggest honors of his career when *Easyriders* magazine presented him with their "Best Fabricated Custom Bike" builder award.

A few months later, the Gibson guitar company invited Dave and fellow builders Donnie Smith and Arlen Ness to design custom bikes to match a specially produced Gibson's anniversary series guitar. The trio of bikes was displayed on national TV and at the Daytona Beach Bike Week gathering in March 2004, and represented more than 75 years of custom motorcycle experience. Though Ness' swingarm chopper, with it's guitar-shaped gas tank, and Smith's cool orange pro-street ride were showstoppers, Perewitz' flamed burgundy chopper, with its guitar-shaped wheel spokes and rock and roll imagery, was clearly the best of the lot.

That's one hell of a journey from his first-ever custom project, which involved Dave accepting a mere $30 to repaint the gas tank on a friend's motorcycle. However, the event proved a turning point for the young custom bike enthusiast who then realized that he could be paid to follow his passion.

Dave actually purchased his first motorcycle as a teenager back in 1967. The rickety 1964 Sportster was quickly torn apart and rebuilt to resemble the lean funky-looking machines Dave had seen other bikers riding around the Boston area. There were botched experiments with homemade chopper front ends, trials and errors involving frame geometry, and enough Bondo putty to cover the ceiling of the Sistine chapel. His first real forays into the chopper scene in the mid-1970s earned him the attention of longtime friend and contemporary Arlen Ness, who shared an appreciation for choppers with dazzling gold inlays, three-dimensional paint, deeply engraved primary and cam covers, and comfortable riding postures rather than radically raked and stretched machines.

The love of being able to ride long distances if necessary on even the most elaborately customized bike remains a priority for Perewitz to this day. His machines all seem to share the same sensibility, one that says bling is great for the ego, but you've got to be able to ride this baby home after the show. Today, the Cycle Fabrications crew includes Dave's son Jesse who is helping out with fabrication and construction duties in the family's new 5,000-square-foot retail sales and

With an eye for elaborate gold-leaf detailing, you can spot a Cycle Fab bike miles away.

A design later copied by former F-1 racer Dan Gurney for his "Alligator" bike, Perewitz' version is all bling, all the time.

service store, alongside daughters Jody and Jaren and Dave's wife, Susan, who serves as shop manager and unofficial den mother.

Unlike many builders who started their careers fabricating small numbers of custom parts and then graduated to full-blown custom motorcycles, Dave is only now beginning to market the billet aluminum cam covers, rocker boxes, and coil mounts that have graced his show machines for the past few years. A serious craftsman, he admits that he only started selling the highly profitable "soft" items such as T-shirts and hats at his family's instance. "I'd rather be building motorcycles," he jokes.

Though the fame and relative fortune are their own rewards, Perewitz experienced the darker side of the chopper scene's runaway popularity when a motorcycle he'd built for a customer was stolen at a New Orleans bike rally. It was the first time he'd lost a machine to the streets, and the experience had clearly shaken the friendly, affable builder. "It's a shame, but the guy I built the bike for never even got to ride it. It was originally built by a shop employee and he never finished it, so a guy called

and said he'd buy it unfinished. We hurried up to get everything completed so we could deliver it to him at the Steel Pony Rundown in New Orleans. We showed it to him in a parking lot of a shop called D.C. Cruisers on the way down and he agreed to buy it, but it disappeared on our first night there," he says, clearly exasperated.

Rather than sit back and wait after seeing several months of hard work disappear, Perewitz employed the help of several of his fellow custom builders who were also in town for the annual rally. It turned out that about 30 other custom motorcycles had disappeared from their trailers during the same weekend. "We went to the cops and they said 'We've had nine murders in town this weekend. Do you really expect we're going to go out looking for your stolen motorcycle?'" Dave recalls.

By conducting their own private investigations into the thefts, the builders managed to discover that an inner-city drug gang was responsible for the massive theft, and many of the bikes were soon recovered as the gang, having no idea just what they'd boosted, sold the bikes back to the eager

Though the Simms name is more widely recognized for fat, low-slung bobbers, this radical longbike proves the depth of the Simms repertoire.

owners for as little as $2,500. It was a weird (and more than a little unsettling) experience for Perewitz and his fellow builders, one he'll not soon forget. "I had the bikes padlocked and chained together and they managed to cut straight through the cable and everything. I eventually managed to get the bike back after a few weeks, so I guess it goes to show that everybody wants a chopper even if they have to steal it," he says, managing a laugh.

RON SIMMS' BAY AREA BAD BOY

One of Ron Simms' favorite roads for testing his newly completed custom bikes runs straight through Hollywood. The Bay Area chopper builder has been in business since the late 1960s, a time, he says wryly, "when you'd get arrested for just trying to ride a chopper in that part of town. It's mind-blowing that, today, I ride one of my bikes down there and everybody loves it."

For Simms, the entire custom chopper movement got its start in this very area, a confluence of small shops and unrecognized metal artists who took a style of motorcycle known only to drag racers and outlaws and made it into a worldwide phenomenon. Simms' father and uncles were all avid bikers, he says, and instead of gathering at a local beer garden or bike shop to see who had the fastest or most stylish machine, it was on display around the Simms household 24-7 as everyone rode their bikes as daily transportation. "This whole custom bike thing got started out here well before I was born, and it's never really been a fad or a novelty for us, it's more a way of life. It's all progressed from this area where we were innovating things years before the rest of the country even saw them," he says.

Simms' first-ever project bike came in the form of a basket-case rolling chassis, sans motor. In a

Additional bracing keeps these 36-inch overstock fork tubes from flexing over road irregularities.

Characterized by a tuff-as-nails 131-cubic-inch "Thug" motor, this Simms bobber is pure Bay Area style.

few months time, using skills he'd picked up helping his father around the family garage, young Ron Simms had cleaned up the old basket case, painted it white with some red flames for style, and even rebuilt the motor. "People would take one look at that bike and the next thing you know, they're asking me to do the same thing to their machines," he says.

Before custom motorcycles became a way of life for Ron Simms, he was dedicated to surfing, a sport at which he'd become very proficient by his late teens. "I used to surf and I worked on bikes to help pay for my surfing habit because I had a bike and people knew I could work on them pretty well. I figured if I worked on enough bikes, I could afford to visit Hawaii where the surfing was great," he recalls. His love of—and proficiency in—fixing motorcycles, however, soon pushed chasing waves from the spotlight.

Though he's watched as styles have come and gone and re-emerged over the years, the basic concept of a Simms custom isn't much different than it was decades ago. The look is a meaty, muscular, and somewhat squat bike, like a pit bull backed with a ferocious, 120-cubic-inch engine. Though Ron Simms has lent his talents to plenty of

Originator of the "taildragger" fender style, this Simms mudguard features an inlaid LED taillight.

longbikes over the years, his signature style is the pro-street dragger, or modern bobber, a distinctive no-bullshit-style of motorcycle he says was derived from street racers in the 1970s.

"They say the chopper got its start out here which is true, but I've always liked the bikes with the big, low look that's almost like a two-wheeled dragster. We've always done our share of old-school bobbers and street rods, and it's neat to look at what we're doing now and compare it to the bikes we were building, say, 25 years ago, and see they're still the same," says Simms.

The shop doesn't just build motorcycles to resemble something that would prove nasty in the quarter mile or would embarrass a Kawasaki Ninja pilot at the stoplights. The line of specially produced "Thug" motors that Simms equips his choppers with are manufactured by S&S and pound out a walloping 140 foot-pounds of torque. The machines are geared so the crest of that tsunami-like power curve occurs just past idling speed, which can result in some neck-snapping stoplight launches or, with an experienced rider, a thick black strip of smoking rubber left in their wake.

The opinionated and plain-spoken Simms says fast, strong-performing choppers are what customers are really looking for in a handmade motorcycle, not Hollywood glitz and glamour. "I guess you can say a large part of our mystique as a shop is that we actually ride our motorcycles, we don't just build them for the TV cameras. We don't have to pretend—if anybody wants to race, they can come here and run against us. I have a mechanic who's been involved in top-fuel drag racing for the past 20 years, and we build all our motorcycles to run," he says.

As a result, the Simms look—one rife with tribal skulls; gangster images straight outta the streets of Oakland, California; and loud, canvas-ripping collector exhausts—is recognizable the world over. Streetfighter fans in Europe and the United Kingdom have cited his eerie paint designs as a major influence, and Simms' shop, located in Hayward, California, was the first to introduce the use of aircraft-grade billet aluminum parts on custom motorcycles back in the early 1980s. The staff now includes several in-house airbrush artists to ensure the bikes all share a similar, unmistakable livery, while a crew of ten fabrication specialists can turn out close to 40 complete motorcycles a year.

The vast, 33,000-square-foot shop has come to resemble the family garage from Simms' childhood, with a feeling of camaraderie shared by the customers and visitors who arrive from all across the country. There's a homey, general-store atmosphere around the place, where talk of motorcycles and rides past, present, and future never goes out of style. The Simms family crew now includes sons Hunter and Dain, the former now helping around the shop at the tender age of 13. Inside the headquarters you'll find Ron's collection of 25 restored vintage motorcycles, a stable that includes rarities such as a 1912 Yale, one of three remaining Harley-Davidson "Silent Grey Fellow" singles, and an Indian board track racer, circa 1919.

Banging the metal and making it run is still paramount for Ron Simms, even though he's sat back and watched the emerging chopper celebrity culture claim several of his closet contemporaries. Still, he'd rather keep it real. "A lot of us guys who've been in the industry a real long time, we're not real happy with what's happened to the business since TV came in. I've turned down enough of the TV stuff to know that motorcycles are not Hollywood and Hollywood is not about motorcycles. They're making it into a fad but I known that, for us, it's still a lifestyle," he says.

ORANGE COUNTY CHOPPERS: LIFE IS LONELY AT THE TOP

Scott Johnson

It was equal parts luck, candor, and personality that landed Paul Teutl Sr. and Jr. a slot on *American Chopper*, the longest-running, and clearly most popular, motorcycle-related TV program to air since the cheesy 1970s crime drama *CHiPs*. Though critics dismiss the program as a slightly scripted combination of *Monster Garage* and the confrontational dysfunctional family drama of *The Jerry Springer Show*, the Teutls have opened up the world of custom two-wheelers to millions who previously ignored motorcycling outright.

During an average broadcast, the family bickers over the construction of one of a series of high-concept show choppers. The formula is simple, but effective. The show's producers always seem to arrive with a "demand" for a completed chopper with only a few days left on the shop's already busy schedule. Wrenches and tantrums are thrown with equal aplomb, and in the end the bike is usually completed, running, and presented to some person or organization to great applause.

While there are detractors within the custom motorcycle community who criticize the Teutls for trivializing the art of building choppers, they maintain an appeal to families everywhere for somehow humanizing the travails that inevitably surface when building choppers in garages both large and small. There's not a mechanic among us who hasn't wanted to choke an assistant at one time or another. When help is provided by family, things can easily become even more maddening.

The fact that a chopper rider can now ride his machine into any mall, downtown area, or suburban township and be treated like a celebrity rather than a felon can be attributed at least partly to reality shows such as *American Chopper* and its precedent, *Motorcycle Mania*. The Teutl family's over-the-top concept bikes may not have the roadworthiness of a Simms machine, or the street cred of a West Coast Chopper, but they have managed to put an approachable human face on choppers, and that's something no one has been able to do to date. Keep on choppin.'

Steve Terry

MILWAUKEE IRON

BUILDER: Randy Simpson

ENGINE: S&S Evolution style

DISPLACEMENT: 107 cubic inches

EXHAUST: Milwaukee Iron tall
organ pipes

TRANSMISSION: Harley-Davidson
5-speed

FORKS: Rolling Thunder springer

CHASSIS: Rolling Thunder rigid

DIMENSIONS: 38-degree rake,
3-inch stretch

SUSPENSION: Rigid

GAS TANK: Milwaukee Iron

FENDERS: Milwaukee Iron

SEAT: Danny Gray

Steve Terry

Steve Terry

Steve Terry

Steve Terry

MILWAUKEE IRON

BUILDER: Randy Simpson

ENGINE: S&S Evolution style

DISPLACEMENT: 96 cubic inches

EXHAUST: Milwaukee Iron dual
drag pipes

TRANSMISSION: Baker 6-speed

FORKS: Paughco springer

CHASSIS: Milwaukee Iron rigid

DIMENSIONS: 35-degree rake,
3-inch stretch

SUSPENSION: Rigid

BLACK HEADHUNTER

LOGIC CYCLES

BUILDER: Rick Hoffman

ENGINE: S&S

DISPLACEMENT: 124 cubic inches

EXHAUST: Samson

TRANSMISSION: Accessories
    Unlimited 6-speed

FORKS: Inverted American
    Suspension,
    12 inches over

CHASSIS: Dakota Thunder

DIMENSIONS: 42-degree rake,
    6 degrees in fork trees

SUSPENSION: Accessories
    Unlimited air-ride

Mike Seate

Mike Seate

Mike Seate

Mike Seate

LOGIC CYCLES
BUILDER: Rick Hoffman
ENGINE: Rev Tech
DISPLACEMENT: 110 cubic inches
EXHAUST: Samson
TRANSMISSION: Rev Tech 6-speed
FORKS: American Suspension inverted, 12 inches over
CHASSIS: RC Components Softail
GAS TANK: Independent
FENDERS: RC Components
SEAT: Ostrich skin, Backside Customs

Simon Green

GIBSON GUITARS CHOPPER

CYCLE FABRICATIONS

BUILDER: Dave Perewitz

ENGINE: Total Performance

DISPLACEMENT: 124 cubic inches

EXHAUST: TCX

TRANSMISSION: Baker 6-speed

FORKS: Joey Perse

CHASSIS: Danny Martin Pro-Street

DIMENSIONS: 40-degree rake,
5-inch stretch

SUSPENSION: Softail

GAS TANK: Perewitz

FENDERS: Perewitz

SEAT: Danny Gray

Simon Green

CYCLE FABRICATIONS

BUILDER: Dave Perewitz

ENGINE: Total Performance

DISPLACEMENT: 121 cubic inches

EXHAUST: TCX

TRANSMISSION: Baker 6-speed

FORKS: Spike

CHASSIS: Daytec Softail

DIMENSIONS: 40-degree rake

SUSPENSION: Softail

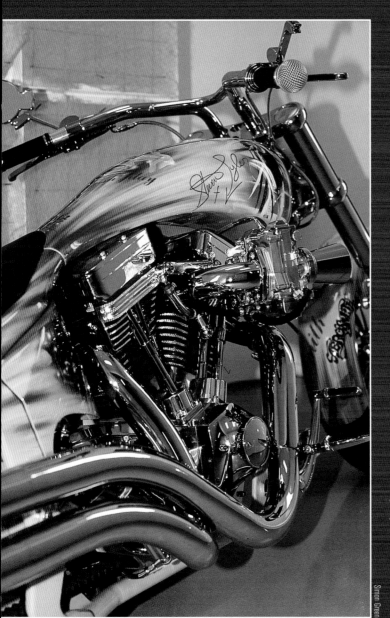

Simon Green

Simon Green

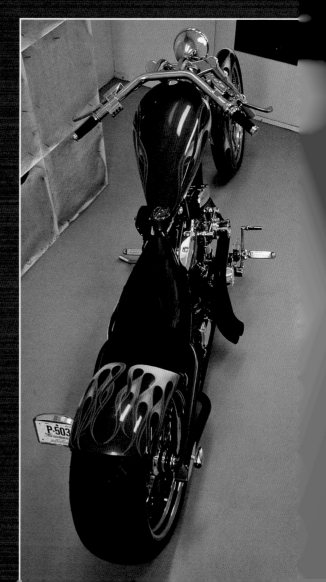

CYCLE FABRICATIONS

BUILDER: Dave Perewitz

ENGINE: Total Performance

DISPLACEMENT: 107 cubic inches

EXHAUST: TCX

TRANSMISSION: Baker 6-speed

FORKS: Joey Perse

CHASSIS: Redneck Engineering

DIMENSIONS: 38-degree rake,
    6-inch stretch

SUSPENSION: Rigid

GAS TANK: Perewitz

FENDERS: Perewitz

SEAT: Danny Gray

Simon Green

Simon Green

Simon Green

CYCLE FABRICATIONS

BUILDER: Dave Perewitz

ENGINE: Total Performance

DISPLACEMENT: 124 cubic inches

EXHAUST: TCX

TRANSMISSION: Baker 6-speed
w/right-side drive

FORKS: Joey Perse

CHASSIS: Daytec Softail

DIMENSIONS: 40-degree rake,
6-inch stretch

SUSPENSION: Softail

GAS TANK: Perewitz

FENDERS: Perewitz

SEAT: Danny Gray

Simon Green

Simon Green

Simon Green

SIMMS CUSTOM CYCLES

BUILDER: Ron Simms

ENGINE: Simms Thug

DISPLACEMENT: 140 cubic inches

EXHAUST: Thunderheader pro-street

TRANSMISSION: Baker 6-speed

FORKS: Ceriani/Storz upside-down

FRAME: Simms/Paughco

DIMENSIONS: 38-degree rake,
  2-inch stretch

GAS TANK: Simms

FENDERS: Simms

SEAT: Corbin

Simon Green

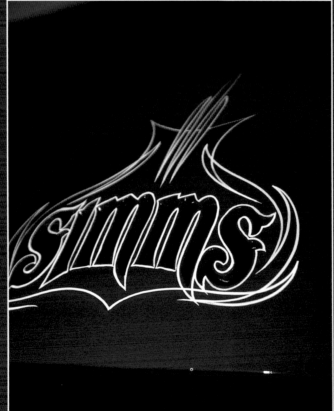

Simon Green

chapter 5

FUTURE SHOCK: CHOPPER STARS OF TOMORROW

Launching your own custom motorcycle shop at this place and time in history could either be the brightest of ideas or a total washout, like attempting to overthrow Harley-Davidson while the Motor Company sits at the top of the big-bike market. Thousands of other custom chopper houses are already in operation, creating countless one-of-a-kind motorcycles and virtually flooding the aftermarket with cleverly designed, eye-pleasing parts. It would take one hell of an imagination, some solid mechanical skills, and a faultless marketing plan (probably all three) to keep afloat in these kinds of treacherous waters. Without a media-friendly image, mile-deep financial backing, or a well-established reputation for creating sought-after choppers, what chance is there of unseating a Billy Lane from the minds of custom bike fans or getting a shop to stock your homemade stretched-steel fenders rather than the tried, true, and roadworthy parts offered by a Rick Doss or Fat Katz? Well, plenty if you listen to some of the newcomers to the chopper game.

Open any enthusiast magazine, from *Hot Bike* to *IronWorks* to *Freeway* and you'll see a burgeoning chopper marketplace hasn't dissuaded many folks from throwing their hats into this already crowded ring. In fact, some of the latest-generation chopper builders say the heightened competition between builders has only made entering the game that much more desirable. Suburban shopping malls now host custom bike shows on weekends the way they once welcomed Boy Scout conventions and teen fashion shows. Chopper shows are also the norm at motorcycle dealerships, regional bike rallies, and drive-in car cruises, all providing new venues for builders looking for an appreciative audience.

Technology has also played a hand with small, unknown chopper fans spreading the word. Where, in times past, a newcomer was charged with getting their motorcycles out on the road to the national chopper show circuit at Daytona, Myrtle Beach, and Sturgis, today a visually compelling Internet site can introduce ideas to a broader public for far less money and hassle.

There's also a lot less hassle in bolting together custom bikes from scratch than gearheads might have faced 20 or 30 years back. Veteran builders who wax poetic about long nights cutting chains to make them fit the longer wheelbases of early choppers or keeping several sets of extended forks around the shop in case something didn't fit are often shocked and more than a little bemused to find that, today, the only must-have tool necessary for owning a chopper is a credit card!

Entire assembly-line firms, or *turn-key* chopper manufacturers as they often like to be called, have sprung up in recent years based solely on the sheer number and variety of custom parts available to modern chopper builders. They can pluck chrome doodads from the pages of a catalog, order softail-style or rigid frames by the dozens, bolt on a pair of billet aluminum CNC-machined wheels and some flashy pattern bodywork, and suddenly, after a few concessions to the D.O.T. such as turn signals and mufflers are added, you've got a chopper.

Some of the better-known forms such as Arizona's Big Dog have become so well-respected in their first full decade of production that their motorcycles are viewed by many as simply alternatives to purchasing a stock Harley-Davidson and outfitting it with scads of bolt-on parts. These tested, refined, and fully warrantied bikes take all the guesswork out of chopper ownership and have become so popular, custom parts suppliers have even started mimicking their assembly-line approach to custom bikes by offering rolling chassis kits and even complete unassembled choppers in a box for the at-home builder.

The audience that aftermarket houses are seeking to attract with their chopper kit bikes is revealed in the sassy über-macho names they apply to these machines; with labels like "Outlaw," "Mastiff" and "Hellcat," they might as well include a dose of extra-strength Viagra with each model!

These machines are handsomely designed, if not incorporating the spontaneity and brazen appeal of a one-off chopper, making them increasingly popular with riders who want to turn up at the local bike meet on something besides a stock Softail Deuce, Honda Valkyrie Rune, or Screamin' Eagle V-Rod, or folks who care more about concepts like proven reliability and extended manufacturer's warranties than owning a bike with one-off sheetmetal parts.

After breaking his back as a competitive snowboarder, Jason Grimes settled on a career as a chopper builder.

Some of the turn-key firms such as Big Dog, Logic, and Carefree Custom Cycles have ventured far beyond the limits (for choppers) of large volume, assembly-line bikes, by updating their range of models with ever more daring and unconventional designs for each model year. Amenities and custom details from seats, paint styles, and frame dimensions can all be special ordered, making these bikes nearly as "custom" as machines being created one at a time, on a single mechanic's light table.

NORTHEAST CHOP SHOP

A deep-seated desire to challenge the competition and express his own singular ideas is what convinced Jason Grimes to open his Northeast Chop Shop in the quiet, frequently snowy hamlet of Portland, Maine. Grimes, a talkative chopper enthusiast, often saw the designs of other builders and imagined himself surpassing what he saw. The former professional snowboarder was, at the tender age of 25, searching for what you might call a less-demanding career after breaking his back during a national snowboarder's competition. After recovering from the fall, Grimes enrolled in the Motorcycle Mechanics Institute in Orlando, Florida, learning the intricacies of Harley-Davidson mechanics from the school's brilliant chief H-D instructor Kim Krummel.

First stop was a Harley-Davidson dealership where Grimes further honed his technical skills. However, not exactly in the way he imagined. "I spent all my time bolting chrome mirrors onto other people's bikes. That wasn't exactly the kind of custom bike building I had in mind," he says with a laugh.

A scant two years later, Grimes was back in his hometown, teaching himself to weld and hand-fabricate steel motorcycle fenders and gas tanks from raw sheetmetal. The shop, at the time, contained little more than a few toolboxes, a used workbench, and Grimes' unbridled ambition; it turned out to be all he'd need to get his start in the chopper game, a world where Northeast Chop Shop is quickly becoming a familiar one.

Grimes himself is mystified by the attraction he has for stripped-down, stretched-out motorbikes. He wasn't even born when many of the engine designs and chopper traditions first saw a stretch of roadway, but he says age, or lack thereof, has no bearing on what he does for a living. "Back when I first started doing service on bikes, people would come to me and ask if I could get them the parts to build them a true custom chopper. I knew when I first went to MMI that my dream was to build bikes like the ones I was always seeing in the magazines because, for some reason, it really intrigued me just like the old muscle cars of the 1960s and 1970s had when I was a kid. I know a lot of guys own sportbikes at my age, but the kind of raw horsepower and feel of a chopper is something different," he says.

Since teaching himself the metalworking fabrication skills he'd need to create one-off gas tanks and fenders, Grimes, along with shop mechanics Doug Rasmuson and Ashley Chase, have completed about 40 ground-up customs. Their style covers everything from sinister-looking, flat-black, neo-bobbers to stretch chops covered in the sort of baroque detail usually found on tattooed bikers or adorning heavy-metal album covers.

Music, whether it's punk, thrash, rap, or metal, provides the shop's quartet of fabricators with much artistic inspiration for the bikes rolling out of Northeast Chop Shop. Look closely and it's evident that the crew frequently incorporates images from their favorite bands and songs into the paint and detailing on the bikes. The green stretch chopper with the dagger-shaped rear fender tip was inspired by rap-metal band Insane Clown Posse. The jester's-head sword tip on the sky-high Fat Katz jockey shifter was actually "borrowed" from a decorative snow globe of all places! While some customers bring in stock Harleys for new bodywork or paint, the shop buzzes loudest when they can design a machine from the ground up with plenty of feedback and crazy, unheard-of ideas from a customer, Grimes says. This was the case with NCS' flat black neo-bobber, which was built to mimic the purposeful look of early hot rod jalopies, right down to the whitewall tires and red wheel trim.

Oddly enough, Grimes is no fan of the well-planed, intricately laid-out custom chopper. All of his designs are pretty much improvised, which means more trial and error than most builders subject themselves to in a lifetime of shop work. "Take the orange chopper, for instance. I was trying to make something that looked long and low, but would ride really well on the kinds of roads we have up here in Maine, something that was very low, compact, and different," says Grimes. "There's so many choppers out there with the same exact rake and stretch and look, and I wanted to do something new, so I played it by ear and never had a game plan at all. Instead, I just tried fitting on different parts as I made them, trying to keep it spontaneous." That way, Grimes says, he doesn't limit his crew in what changes or alterations they can make to a bike in progress—if they don't care for the lines of a fender or the way a custom seat pan lays on a frame, they're free to trash that particular part as long as they're willing to invest the labor in making a suitable replacement. It's a time-consuming

Tommy Imperati of Tommy Gun Choppers on one of his recent creations. The block-long beast rolls on a front-end 36 inches overstock, but years of experience means the bike has no front-end flop or slow steering.

process, which can stretch the build of a full-blown NCS chopper out as long as three or four months, but well worth it, the owner says.

"It's not like you see on TV where I can work with a drawing or a blueprint and get everything done in a big hurry with people looking over my shoulder telling me to hurry up all the time. I know some customers want stuff fast, but when I'm building a chopper, time can't really be a factor if you want it done right."

✝OMMY GUN CHOPPERS

When it comes to unique, custom motorcycle workshops, or unique personalities, you'd have to search a long time to outdo Tom Imperati, the mind behind Branford, Connecticut's Tommy Gun Choppers. Take a walk through this small, family-operated business

and you'll be just as likely to stub your toe on the disassembled innards of an old Browning .50 caliber belt-fed machine gun as you would a motorcycle engine casing. Outside in the tiny parking lot, custom choppers with glistening chrome springer forks are parked next to antique troop carriers, jeeps, and Army-issue Harley-Davidson 45 side valve twins that look like they just rolled in from the beaches at Normandy. The workshop's walls, where most motorcycle shops would be content to hang cheesecake parts calendars, are covered in what looks like the prop room from *Hogan's Heroes*. Vintage WWII military helmets, uniforms, and even a few decommissioned hand grenades, serve as both decorations and proof that Imperati's obsession with choppers and militaria is on lock and load.

But for all the devotion to warfare's toolbox, Imperati is a jovial, fun-loving, bear of a man, the sort of guy who will pause work for a quick joke and still enjoys working alongside his 73-year-old mother and 77-year-old aunt on a daily basis. The two women, like Imperati himself, switch duties from the shop's gunsmithing business to the procurement of custom motorcycle parts. His everyday streetbike, naturally, is an eardrum-bender of a drag bike, replete with a fire-breathing 131-cubic-inch Merch Performance racing motor pulsing out 160 horsepower through a fat 300-mm tire.

For someone known as a relative newcomer to the chopper game, Imperati actually started building motorcycles as a hobby back in 1980. At the time, he recalls, not many riders in the Northeast cared about running streetbikes with radically raked and extended front ends or rigid suspension. There were still plenty of custom parts left lying around the back rooms of local bike shops, however, and they could be had cheap. He started building choppers as "something to do when I got tired of fooling around with guns."

Today, Tommy Gun Choppers completes around two dozen custom bike projects annually, including high-performance engine work involving big-inch stroker kits and the occasional supercharger. Guns or bikes, it all seems to make little difference to Imperati, who enjoys his work like a kid buzzing through a scale-model kit on Christmas morning. There's a strong sense of playfulness in his work, evidenced by wacky designs, including three-dimensional metal flames welded to the gas tanks of some Tommy Gun Choppers. He's become adept enough with a plasma cutter in recent years that Imperati recently designed a fender for one of his rigid stretch chops that appeared to have been torn in half—jagged edges and all—by a 800-pound gorilla. It's a startling piece of eye-candy for a chopper, part of the shop's insistence on outdoing the competition with ever-crazier ideas.

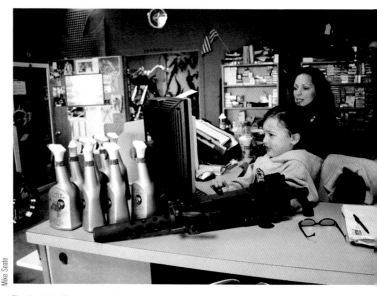

Mike Seate

That's Little Tommy and Mom at work in Imperati's fascinating shop, which combines military history, a cigar store, and custom chopper workshop under one roof!

"It's so different from back when I started. Back then, people either loved choppers or hated them. You'd build one and people would stare at it and compliment you just because of the way the thing looked or how hard those old longbikes were to ride. But now with so many guys doing it, the bikes are far more high-tech than they used to be," he says.

The biggest change Tommy Gun has seen in the chopper field concerns the way molding—that weird and highly difficult application of fiberglass Bondo putty used to smooth over seams and imperfections in metal parts—has suddenly almost vanished from view. Today, Imperati says, technology dictates the use of new welding processes using brass and bronze rods, electrostatic powder coating, and heat-treated finishes to make a beautiful and roadworthy chopper. Today, he's powder coating tons of chopper parts from frames to even gas tanks and hasn't touched a can of Bondo in more than a decade. "There's no Bondo at all because the welding is done with bronze and brass rods and this makes

A CNC milling machine was used to etch the shop's Tommy Gun logo into the frame gusset. Careful pulling that gas cap!

things a lot smoother after you hit the seams with a 3-M wheel. And unlike Bondo, which will melt if you try and throw hot powder coat over it, this stuff looks great and holds up to anything, but you really have to be up on your game to do it properly," he says.

Yes, that's a real Thompson .45 caliber automatic pressed into duty as a coil. A real WWII bayonet serves as shifter linkage.

And being on his game means pulling out wacky ideas like the olive drab chopper Tommy Gun built to commemorate his family's involvement in the U.S. airborne corps during WWII. Maybe commemorate isn't the right word. Perhaps this machine, with an actual .45 caliber Thomson sub-machine gun mounted on one of the stretched frame's downtubes, an actual 20-mm anti-aircraft shell for a throttle grip, and a German Wermacht dagger handle forced into duty as a clutch lever, is more an unfettered, almost boyish, celebration of the WWII era. It's also one of the most over-the-top original choppers to come down the road in years. Imperati, who is accustomed to repairing vintage tanks, half-tracks, and, yes, motorcycles for friends and military collectible fans, says the army-surplus parts mounted to the paratrooper chopper are genuine 1940s vintage, including the German potato-masher hand grenades mounted as forward-control footpegs and the twin bayonets that form the sissy bar.

He also builds a mean black stretch chopper and the odd bobber, complete with old-school apehangers, tiny peanut gas tanks, and blacked-out shotgun pipes. And though the crew at Tommy Gun Choppers is hip to new developments in the aftermarket such as six-speed close-ratio transmissions and air-ride suspension systems, he still prefers the hard ride and simple mechanics of an old-style 1960s chopper. "I've always thought a cool chopper had more to do with fabrication and unique stuff than all that high-tech stuff you see today. The really

An Army-issue fire extinguisher is bolted beneath the stretched King Sportster gas tank while a functioning Tommy Gun is mounted to the forward downtubes.

A genuine WWII paratrooper's helmet adorns the rear fender of Tommy's 101st Airborne chopper.

expensive parts cost so much and I've always thought you don't really need a bunch of money to make a bike look cool. You just need imagination" he says.

With the welding torch out and his mind racing, Imperati is the true mad wizard in his workshop; his eyes seem to glaze over and he works the bare frame of his project bike from front to rear, studying the chassis lines, and forming imaginary parts with his hands in the air as he starts the sheetmetal fabrication process.

Not one to work much with drawings, blueprints, or computer-aided drafting, Imperati is more the hands-on type. When a part he pounds out of metal doesn't please his eye, it's not unknown for him to tear it from an unfinished bike for a trip to the backyard where its blasted full of holes with one of his vintage rifles. "I know I've been said to take way too much time on my projects, but sometimes I'll just sit there and look at the frame and think of something for a couple of hours and I'll put things on and take them off again.

"You can't do this in a hurry."

SINKHOLE CUSTOMS: CHOPPERS, FARM RAISED

Brent Nevil was happy with his career as a peanut and cotton farmer in Statesboro, Georgia. A competent and trained mechanic, Nevil could easily repair his own farming equipment and harvesting machinery, and with his wife, Ginger, a hard-working co-owner of the family farm, he still had time left to ride and create unique parts for his favorite motorcycle.

But working on combine harvesters and tractors is only so much fun, especially when your riding buddies are constantly bugging you to hang up the pitchfork and pick up a welding torch. "I guess you could say we're just people who always wanted something more. We'd been riding bikes together for years and Brent has been into choppers his whole life," Ginger says. "They say we're the type of people who are never satisfied because we always want the biggest, baddest, and best, or something that's fairly outside the norm." For the Nevil clan, that meant farming only part time as they launched Sinkhole Customs (named after the various sinkholes dotting the countryside near their farm) in the spring of 2004.

Because there weren't many choppers on the road in their area, and even fewer custom shops where a customer could have a custom bike built to their specifications, the Nevils saw a sinkhole of their own, right in the middle of a growing motorcycle scene, one that was just waiting for the kind of high-end motorcycles the couple now builds and sells. As in many areas of the country, Ginger Nevil says Georgia riders tend to customize their stock bikes rather than build choppers because they're afraid of the exorbitant insurance costs and high theft rate for choppers. But with long, straight, and very smooth roads, and a riding season that lasts somewhere around nine months, Georgia's chopper scene is slowly starting to take off. Building a machine that will handle as well as it looks is one of Sinkhole's main goals, and they tend to design their bikes around a moderately raked chassis (no more than 40 degrees of rake) to ensure a steady ride and no front-end flop.

Ginger built and designed the funky green-and-yellow John Deere Tractors chopper herself over the span of six months, incorporating the Deere factory's wildlife logo into the cut primary cover, and detailing the bike with a custom yellow coil cover and matching one-piece V-shaped handlebars. The

machine, built in honor of the family's three successive generations of farmers, earned the pair a spot on the cover of *Street Chopper* magazine and has been taking home show trophies throughout the South. The bike has proven so popular, they've received several requests to build similar choppers for customers.

Right now, the pair is focusing their considerable skills on designing and then marketing a series of billet wheels, bodywork, and seats, and they're willing to put together partially completed rolling chassis kits for riders with a DIY mindset. Like many builders, Ginger says most customers have an unrealistic idea of how much trial, error, and just plain time is consumed by a chopper project. "People always ask me what the biggest problems are in building a bike like this and, beyond a doubt, it's dealing with parts distributors and trying to relay information and specifications about what parts you need to someone thousands

Hand-rendered, three-dimensional chrome detailing on the gas tank of Ginger Nevil's chopper—nice!

As the owner of a working soy bean farm, Brent Nevil's love of John Deere tractors is revealed in this clever green and yellow chopper's primary cover.

well-known shops that are milking the market for every dollar they can get. What we're more into is getting a foundation in parts sales, which is hard against some of the Internet guys who don't really even have shops and have no overhead. But this is a love my husband and I both have, and we get a large sense of gratification making stuff with our hands, and my favorite part is the metal work, which is where you can really express yourself," she says.

The sinewy, even luxurious, range chopper from Sinkhole is a prime example of the work the couple is quickly becoming known for. The chromed tribal decoration on the 4-gallon Independent gas tank was done in-house, along with the while the fenders that were cut from sheetmetal blanks and hand-turned on an English wheel to contour around the rear wheel.

of miles away. You'll have this burning idea you really want to get finished, but you end up waiting and waiting on some small parts to come in or waiting on a painter or chromer," she says. After years of repairing farm machinery, Ginger and Brent find the comparatively clean small-scale work of building choppers a breeze, even sharing in the bare metal mock-up phase, wiring, and troubleshooting stages of each build.

The Nevils know they've entered the chopper market at a time when its more crowded and, at times, crazier than a bench-clearing brawl on the pitcher's mound, but they're confident their mechanical and artistic ability will keep them abreast of the game. "The size of the custom bike market at the moment actually makes it easier for us because there are so many builders out there and there are a lot of them who have

Radical frame stretch on this Sinkhole Customs chopper makes for a wild ride and even wilder profile; it also helps make room for a stump-pulling 124-cubic-inch S&S motor.

The Nevils have plans to expand their parts line to include the large-diameter billet aluminum handlebars with internal wiring, tribal coil mounts, custom shifter rods and linkage, all within the next four or five years. In between planting and tending crops, that is. "There's not many people who can do what they love for a living. There are easier ways to make a living, but at least this has always been fun and a real challenge to see what we can come up with," Ginger says.

NORTH HILLS CYCLE: GIRL POWER

At an age when most of Sara Liberte's girlfriends were designing prom dresses and painting their nails for weekend dates, she had other plans. As a self-confessed tomboy who enjoyed hanging around her father Dave's Southbridge, Massachusetts,

steel fabrication shop, Sara's nails were most likely caked with engine grease and her weekend social schedule filled with carburetor rebuilds and welding lessons. Today, at the ripe young age of 29, Liberte is co-owner of North Hills Cycle, a Pittsburgh-area custom motorcycle business she runs with partner Ron Tonetti. And those long weekends in Dad's steelyard have helped Liberte forge her way into a rare position for a woman: she actually designs and builds custom motorcycles, a job most people imagine to be far beyond the abilities of females. "When people hear I'm part of a bike shop, they always ask if I'm the secretary, or they assume that I do all the office paperwork. I guess there's just not that many women doing what I do," she says with a characteristically modest shrug.

Sara's pursuit of a career in sheetmetal fabrication and chopper building might have shocked even her

"Most guys think I'm a secretary or bookkeeper at the shop, but I get my hands dirty," says Sara Liberte.

Sara Liberte learned the basics of mechanical engineering from her family. From there, she took to choppers on her own.

gearhead father and brother Craig, but the Liberte family's background is deeply rooted in mechanics. The clan frequently restored and customized classic hot rods and muscle cars, and Sara received a basket case 1966 Ford Mustang for a 16th birthday present. "It needed a lot of T.L.C. and some mechanical tweaking, so my father and brother taught me a lot about how to work on engines and enjoy getting my hands dirty," she said.

After sharing an ATV bike with her brother during adolescence, Sara said she was surprised when the family put the boot down when she expressed an interest in streetbikes. "They liked cars and fast hot rods, but my mother had a friend killed riding a motorcycle years before, so they were scared that I'd get killed or seriously hurt," she says.

Nevertheless, after leaving college where she earned a degree in photography, Sara divested her savings and ended up with a rough-condition 1978 Harley-Davidson XLCR Café Racer. The bike, once owned by New England's custom bike king Dave Perewitz, was in need of some careful going over. "The bike had been in storage for years and the

fork lock was stuck in place and the owner had no key for it. I remember how, at five-foot-four and one hundred pounds, I couldn't even pick the thing up at first because it was so top-heavy," she recalls. But after shedding the rusty lock with a set of bolt-cutters, Sara rebuilt the old Café Racer's electrical system, cleaned it up, and started on her lifelong obsession with improving upon Milwaukee's in-house designs.

She credits much of her acumen and skill to the generosity of the custom bike builders she's studied under. Before leaving Massachusetts in the 1990s, Sara spent time lugging wrenches at a small shop owned by Canadian biker Mark L'herux with whom she credits with teaching her the ins and outs of the art of chopper building and the daily intricacies of running a functioning, profitable motorcycle shop. While photographing motorcycles at the annual Laconia Rally a few years later, Sara met her current partner Ron Tonetti, who had already begun his own custom motorcycle career in Pennsylvania. Before long, she'd packed up and headed to Pittsburgh where the two pooled their resources and opened their shop in April 1999.

Today, Sara spends her days at North Hills Cycle covering everything from parts orders to computer-drafting sheetmetal parts and custom paint schemes. With Ron as principal builder and spray-gun wizard, the shop's busy work bays have turned out an interesting cross-section of hand-built Hogs during its first five years in business. Regular *IronWorks* readers may recall a bold, sinewy, yellow-and-blue Paul Yaffe kit chopper in those pages last year built by North Hills Cycle to a shelf-full of show trophies while, more recently, Sara says she struggled to avoid following trends while still pumping out original and highly desirable motorcycles.

They recently completed a Jesse James kit bike, done up in a raw, unadorned, flat black and rawhide finish, replete with a primer-colored chassis and a gas tank with glow-in-the-dark green flames. The stealth treatment seems to be what the rawboned rigid chopper was screaming for. The project was a joint effort between Sara and Ron, as are all their custom bikes. "We did a lot of stuff together and neither one of us will do anything without each other. We sometimes run into a total clash of ideas to come up with something we both like, but after so long, we always end up with something we're proud of," she says.

Young and hip enough to be into diverse custom biking trends such as Europe's burgeoning street-fighter craze, Sara's design for their futuristic red lowrider Buell has garnered some serious industry attention, forging what appears to be a blend between an American-made sportbike and a pavement-scraping boulevard bike. Together, the pair manages to complete about five to seven full custom motorcycles each year alongside a shed-load of routine maintenance work and lots of smaller bolt-on projects for their growing list of regular customers. With so many choppers in the public eye, Sara said she's been deluged with requests to make stock Harleys look more like the sort of motorcycles seen on TV. And while there's a real temptation to jump on the "long forks, big motors" bandwagon, she'd much rather focus on her own unique vision.

"I want our work to always be clean, uncluttered, and mechanically sound. That's what really sets things apart," she says. "People almost expect a female builder to be all into flashy pretty bikes that don't run, but it's very important for us to make sure the mechanical integrity of the motorcycles is there and that the frame geometry is solid so they run well."

Simon Green

Simon Green

Simon Green

NORTHEAST CHOP SHOP

BUILDER: Jason Grimes

ENGINE: Harley-Davidson

DISPLACEMENT: 80 cubic inches

EXHAUST: NCS

TRANSMISSION: Harley-Davidson
   5-speed

FORKS: Accutronix/Frank's,
   10 inches over

CHASSIS: Chopper Guyz

DIMENSIONS: 40-degree rake,
   6-inch stretch

SUSPENSION: Rigid

GAS TANK: Independent

FENDERS: Russ Weinemont

SEAT: NCS

WHEELS: RC Components,
   (rear) 18 x 8.5,
   (front) 21 x 2.25

GREEN INSANE CLOWN CHOPPER

Simon Green

Simon Green

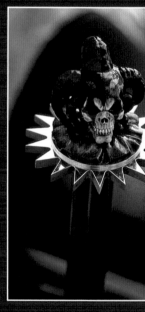

NORTHEAST CHOP SHOP

BUILDER: Jason Grimes

ENGINE: Revtech, show-polished

DISPLACEMENT: 88 cubic inches

EXHAUST: Paul Yaffe original

TRANSMISSION: RevTech
5-speed

FORKS: Billet Concepts with
Pro-One lower legs

CHASSIS: Santee rigid

DIMENSIONS: 43-degree rake,
6-inch backbone stretch,
4-inch downtubes

SUSPENSION: None

GAS TANK: NCS

FENDERS: NCS

SEAT: NCS

WHEELS: RC Components Wicked
billet wheels, (rear) 18 x 5.5,
(front) 21 x 2.25

Simon Green

Simon Green

Simon Green

NORTHEAST CHOP SHOP

BUILDER: Jason Grimes

ENGINE: Rev Tech

DISPLACEMENT: 100 cubic inches

EXHAUST: Hooker 2-into-1 collector

TRANSMISSION: Rev Tech 6-speed

FORKS: Paughco Springer, 4 inches over

CHASSIS: Santee

DIMENSIONS: 35-degree rake, 2-inch stretch

SUSPENSION: Rigid

GAS TANK: NCS

FENDERS: NCS

SEAT: NCS

WHEELS: RC Components Warlock, powder

Courtesy of Tommy Gun Choppers

Courtesy of Tommy Gun Choppers

TOMMY GUN CHOPPERS

BUILDER: Tom Imperati

ENGINE: Shovelhead

DISPLACEMENT: 113 cubic inches

EXHAUST: Handmade shotgun drags

TRANSMISSION: Harley-Davidson
4-speed

FORKS: Pro One

CHASSIS: Tommy Gun

DIMENSIONS: 39-degree rake,
4-inch stretched downtubes

SUSPENSION: Rigid

GAS TANK: Tommy Gun sporty,
modified

FENDERS: Rear cut from two
separate Chica fenders

SEAT: Barrett Designs

WHEELS: American Wire,
(front) 21 x 2.25, (rear) 16 x 150mm

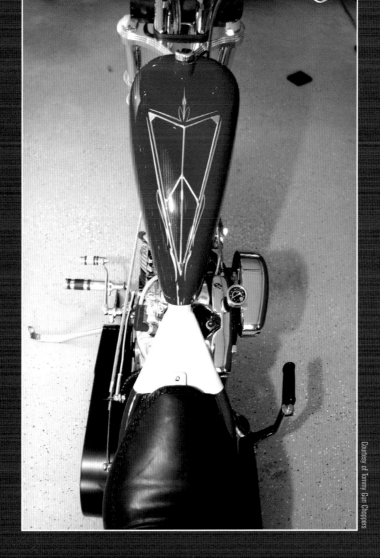

Courtesy of Tommy Gun Choppers

Courtesy of Tommy Gun Choppers

TOMMY GUN CHOPPERS

BUILDER: Tom Imperati

ENGINE: S&S

DISPLACEMENT: 100 cubic inches

EXHAUST: Wicked Bros.

TRANSMISSION: 5-speed Accessories Unlimited

FORKS: Eddie Trotta, 14 inches over

CHASSIS: Eddie Trottta single-downtube

DIMENSIONS: 40-degree rake, 6-inch upward stretch

SUSPENSION: None

GAS TANK: Tommy Gun

SEAT: Tommy Gun

WHEELS: Extreme Machine billet

Courtesy of Tommy Gun Choppers

Courtesy of Tommy Gun Choppers

Courtesy of Tommy Gun Choppers

Courtesy of Tommy Gun Choppers

TOMMY GUN CHOPPERS

BUILDER: Tom Imperati

ENGINE: Merch Performance Racing

DISPLACEMENT: 120 cubic inches

EXHAUST: Tommy Gun

TRANSMISSION: Accessories
Unlimited 6-speed

FORKS: Paughco springer,
4 inches over

CHASSIS: Chopper Guys

DIMENSIONS: 38-degree rake

SUSPENSION: None

GAS TANK: Fat Katz stretched fatbobs

FENDERS: Tommy Gun

SEAT: Tommy Gun

WHEELS: High Tech, (rear) 18 x 4.5,
(front) 21

BRENT'S SINKHOLE CHOPPER

Steve Terry

Steve Terry

SINKHOLE CUSTOMS

BUILDER: Brent Nevil

ENGINE: Total Performance

DISPLACEMENT: 124 cubic inches

EXHAUST: Wicked Bros.

TRANSMISSION: Powerhouse
6-speed

FORKS: RC Components
inverted, 16 inches over

CHASSIS: Carolina Customs

DIMENSIONS: 43-degree rake,
8-inch stretch

SUSPENSION: Softail

GAS TANK: Independent

FENDERS: Fat Katz/Sinkhole

SEAT: Bowen Upholstery

WHEELS: RC Components
(rear) 18 x 250,
(front) 21 x 2.25

Steve Terry

Steve Terry

Steve Terry

Steve Terry

SINKHOLE CUSTOMS

BUILDER: Ginger Nevil

ENGINE: Total Performance

DISPLACEMENT: 124 cubic inches

EXHAUST: Wicked Bros.

TRANSMISSION: Powerhouse 6-speed

FORKS: Sinkhole 10 inches over

CHASSIS: Carolina Customs

DIMENSIONS: 40-degree rake,
    6-inch stretch

SUSPENSION: Legends air-ride

GAS TANK: Jesse James Villain

FENDERS: Sinkhole/Redneck

SEAT: Jerry's Upholstery

WHEELS: Covington's Cycle City
    Sinners, (rear) 18 x 250,
    (front) 21 x 2.25

YELLOW
PAUL YAFFE
CHOPPER

Chaz Palla

NORTH HILLS CYCLE

BUILDER: Ron Tonetti/Sara Liberte

ENGINE: Rev Tech

DISPLACEMENT: 100 cubic inches

EXHAUST: Yaffe Crack Pipes

TRANSMISSION: Rev Tech 6-speed

FORKS: Paughco 10 inches over

CHASSIS: Yaffe softail

DIMENSIONS: 40-degree rake,
    6-inch stretch

SUSPENSION: Legends air-ride

GAS TANK: Paul Yaffe Zombie

FENDERS: Yaffe

SEAT: North Hills

WHEELS: Paul Yaffe Originals,
    18 inches rear, 21 inches front

SPECIAL FEATURES: Molded bodywork

Chaz Palla

Mike Seate

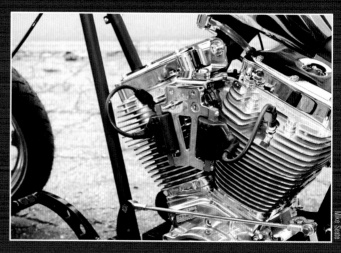

Mike Seate

NORTH HILLS CYCLE

BUILDER: Ron Tonetti/Sara Liberte

ENGINE: S&S

DISPLACEMENT: 117 cubic inches

EXHAUST: West Coast Choppers Hell Bent

TRANSMISSION: Rev Tech 5-speed

FORKS: Perse

CHASSIS: Jesse James C.F.L.

DIMENSIONS: 38-degree rake, 4-inch stretch

SUSPENSION: None

GAS TANK: West Coast Villain

FENDERS: Jesse James, modified

SEAT: North Hills

WHEELS: West Coast, (rear) 18 inches (front) 21 inches

Sara Liberte

Sara Liberte

Sara Liberte

NORTH HILLS CYCLE
BUILDER: Ron Tonetti/Sara Liberte
ENGINE: S&S
DISPLACEMENT: 113 cubic inches
EXHAUST: Samson
TRANSMISSION: Baker 6-speed
FORKS: Paughco springer
CHASSIS: Daytec softail
DIMENSIONS: 34-degree rake
SUSPENSION: Legends air-ride
GAS TANK: Fat Katz
FENDERS: Fat Katz
SEAT: North Hills
WHEELS: (rear) 18-inch Performance
Machine solid, (front) 21-inch
American Wire

İNDEX

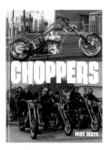
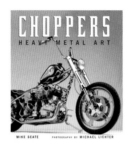
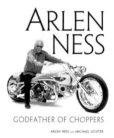
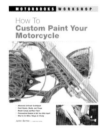
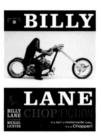
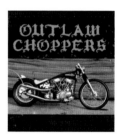